Paradigms and Parables:

The Ten Commandments for Ethics in Business

Brother Louis DeThomasis, FSC
President
St. Mary's University of Minnesota

Bill Ammentorp
Professor
University of Minnesota

Human Resource Development Press, Inc.
Amherst, Massachusetts

Published by Human Resource Development Press, Inc.
22 Amherst Road
Amherst, Massachusetts 01002
1-800-822-2801

Copyright © 1995 by Brother Louis DeThomasis, FSC and Bill Ammentorp

All rights reserved. No part of this publication may be reproduced or transmitted in any form or by any means, electronic or mechanical, including photocopying, recording, or any information storage and retrieval system, without permission in writing from the publisher.

ISBN 0-87425-998-3

Production Services by Susan Kotzin
Editorial Services by Michael J. Burke
Cover Design by Old Mill Graphics

CONTENTS

Introduction 1

Chapter 1 Paradigms and Parables:
           Managing Change in the Nineties 5

Chapter 2 Talking the Talk: Social Justice 19

Chapter 3 The Parable of Ethical Action 27

Chapter 4 The Parable of Corporate Justice 35

Chapter 5 The Parable of Technology 45

Chapter 6 The Parable of the Junk Bonds:
           Doing Ethics in Business 55

Chapter 7 The Parable of Stewardship:
           Faith and Finance 63

Chapter 8 The Parable of Individuality: One Body 71

Chapter 9 The Parable of Despair:
           Economics, Opportunity, and Social Justice . . 77

Chapter 10 The Parable of the Gift:
           In Search of Extravagance 87

Chapter 11 The Parable of Ethics: One World 93

References 99

Appendix 103

INTRODUCTION

Our work as educators and consultants has taken us into the lives of countless business men and women. We have worked with many in joint business ventures and watched as our students have taken positions of leadership in public- and private-sector organizations. Over the years, we have come to feel that America has lost its way in the pursuit of individual gain and short-term, bottom-line objectives. We have the sense that our nation now stands at the height of its economic power, not fully confident in the human value of the capitalist system.

Our uncertainty is manifest in many present-day social and economic conditions. An America of growth and wealth tolerates, and often ignores, growing misery in its midst. Our products, once the standard of excellence in the world, come in second best to those of other countries. Political decisions made in the name of our Constitution create untold human havoc in third-world nations. These are, it seems to us, indications of business and political leadership that is unsure of its ethical foundations, the products of decision makers who do the expedient rather than consider the long-run social impact of their behavior. We are a nation whose ethical direction is dictated by the voices of interest groups; a country where the values of humanity and social purpose have given way to greed and a cult of the individual.

We are clearly not alone in coming to this conclusion. The proliferation of papers, textbooks, and courses dealing with business ethics is testimony to the fact that many of our intellectual and business leaders feel the need for guideposts to chart the course of economic life. While we agree wholeheartedly with these developments, we find them short of the mark in that they fail to capture the imagination of business men and women. They attempt to teach by example, which often leaves readers baffled as to how they might behave as ethical business leaders.

This book is an attempt to address this shortcoming. It is written for business women and men who are troubled by the ethical implications of their day-to-day work. It is a book that asks for the commitment of business leaders to the attainment of social and economic justice in all nations. In making the case for justice as a business goal, we have intentionally made use of several familiar religious metaphors. By framing ethical issues in religious terms like commandments, parables, and sermons, we hope to convince readers that individual commitment to the ideal of justice when coupled with collective responsibility for its achievement is the *only* viable basis for business activity in the years ahead.

Paradigms and Parables enables business men and women to make a quantum leap from the discussion of business ethics to action. The Ten Commandments for Doing Ethics in Business presented in the pages that follow are more than mere exhortations. They draw on an analysis of the social and economic fabric of business life to show the reader how individual actions can add to, or detract from, the lives of others. In the parables, we have used an ancient teaching modality that leaves an image of ethical behavior in the mind of the reader so that there is always a visual reference point for business decisions.

Paradigms and Parables is not, however, a reference book for those facing ethical problems. It can only be a help for business leaders in clarifying the issues involved in their daily activities. If its readers come away with a heightened understanding of the moral imperative of social and economic justice and a sense of their own responsibility for its attainment, the book will be a success.

This is not to say that *Parables* can stand alone as a guide to all management behavior. Business leaders cannot approach the turbulent times of the nineties clothed only in ethical purity. They must also be informed practitioners who know their own business as well as the world setting in which each must compete. In another book, *The Transformal Organization,* we have attempted to outline the framework in which ethical management must take place. It is ethics *together* with wisdom that will make capitalism shine across the globe in the years ahead.

As readers proceed through this book, we hope they will perceive the many faults of our capitalist system. The reader may, as too many other business leaders have, despair of attaining justice within the bounds of our economic system. For them, we emphasize the fact that the capitalist system is the only proven form of economic organization. After all is said, we remain confirmed capitalists, secure in our faith in the potential for ethical action on the part of all those who participate in economic life. Together, we can create a world where the goals of economic and social justice are realized for all people.

Brother Louis DeThomasis, FSC	Bill Ammentorp
Saint Mary's University of Minnesota	University of Minnesota
Winona, MN	Minneapolis, MN
October 1993	

CHAPTER 1

Paradigms and Parables: Managing Change in the Nineties

In the decade of the 1980s, Americans sowed the seeds of the problems we face in the nineties. It was a time when the United States borrowed its way to prosperity; when many of our cities became urban wastelands; when the public lost confidence in its business and political leaders. When these seeds sprouted, they rapidly matured to create a business environment where traditional ideas and ways of managing no longer work. Old concepts such as leverage have been redefined to fit a business climate in which buyouts have replaced growth. Profitability and productivity have been set at odds by competition from other cultures where these terms have very different meanings.

Developments like these lead to a widespread belief that something is wrong with the American system and that a new form of management thinking is required in order to put the American dream back on track. These feelings have resulted in a wide range of attempts by professors, speakers, and writers to define the principles that should guide decision makers. These well-intentioned people have produced a bewildering array of pamphlets, books, and courses in which the rules of business practice have been set down.

The traveling manager can see the fruits of these labors at any airport bookstall. There are countless self-help pamphlets telling "how it was" at a particular company. There are others that make the claim that some historical figure—like Genghis Khan—was the last person to "get it right." As the traveler wades through this slough of platitudes, there is often the experience that something is missing. And it is. There are few writers who take the trouble to explore what is "right" for business in the nineties. We find no restatement of the values underlying the American dream and no general principles of ethical behavior against which managers might measure their actions.

The absence of ethical approaches to management is not an accident. The complexity of modern business, finance, and government would require an ethical code of encyclopedic proportions and a cadre of ethical lawyers to interpret every decision and action. Everyone involved in business also knows that behavior is more effectively controlled by the beliefs and values of each person, and that rules and punishment are poor substitutes for shared principle.

In effect, nobody can "do ethics for business." Ethical conduct must be defined in practice, and business leaders must look into themselves for the solutions to the problems of the times. This requires a shared sense of purpose and a consensus as to the standards whereby individual actions and organizational outcomes can be judged. We all need a clear understanding of what our economic and social systems are about and what impact they have on the individuals whose lives they touch. For ethics is about money and power and how the use of these resources changes the quality of life of citizens, workers, and consumers.

Ethical behavior is that which improves the lot of everyone involved. As Albert Schweitzer has stated, "In a general sense, ethics is the name we give to our concern for good behavior. We feel an obligation to consider not only our own personal well-being, but also that of others and of human society as a whole." This definition is a timeless statement of principle in a global society where the consequences of business and governmental decisions are often worldwide in scope. It brings all of mankind under one overarching objective:

Act so that the largest number of people receive the maximum benefit from every decision and action.

When we put this definition to work in a global context, we are confronted with issues that have never before faced the business community. They are not the superficial issues national financial management; nor are they the splashy problems of insider trading, corporate raiding, or executive lifestyle. They are the fundamental issues of life and death for millions of people.

These issues take shape in some very basic questions. Who will be able to earn even a subsistence level of living? Who may work with dignity despite race or belief? Who will own and use land and other scarce resources? To what purpose? Who will have the power to decide how these questions will be addressed? And who will evaluate the answers provided by business and government?

It's the Acceleration, Stupid!

The answers to these questions are to be found in our understanding of change. For all of history, business and political leaders have gauged their success in terms of their capacity to anticipate change and to cope with its consequences. And, so long as change was slow and predictable, decision makers were able to reform their organizations and practices to accommodate new realities. This is no longer the case—because the pace of change can no longer be measured in decades. Instead, change is accelerating and rapidly outdistancing our expertise and experience. *It's the acceleration, stupid!*

Accelerating change makes every decision an important one. There is no time to experiment with a new idea, policy, or product; action either stands up to change, or doesn't. It's even more important to note that we cannot insulate management from the global character of change. With every turn of our networked world, it is increasingly obvious that those who decide about the use of money and power control the destiny of humanity: who eats; who starves; who is sick; who is well; who lives with dignity; who exists in hopelessness.

For most of recorded history, we have left these problems to our churches and our governments. We have asked the church to channel some of our resources to the less fortunate. And we have encouraged many to live lives of service in order to better the human condition. Government, too, has been seen as a mechanism to alleviate suffering by enacting and funding policies that will provide specific services to those with demonstrated need.

All of which worked fairly well in the relatively stable past. Now these institutions cannot stand alone in the face of accelerating change.

Church and government remain as key actors in the global society. But they are dwarfed by the scope, power, and *responsiveness* of modern business. The ball is now in the court of business men and women and it is their actions that will determine the quality of life of humanity. The burden falls most heavily on democratic capitalists because they are at the center of the global business network where decisions made in Tokyo today will determine employment patterns in St. Louis and Mexico City tomorrow.

The business practices of democratic capitalism have taken over world finance. They have been used to organize production in even the least-developed countries. And they have provided a system of rewards in which risk and productivity are central to the life chances of everyone. We have today what Peter Drucker calls a "transnational economy" where the measures of success cut across the lines drawn by governments and traditional value systems.

But, in its striving to become the dominant world system, democratic capitalism has sown the seeds of potential failure. It is its own worst enemy.

"We Have Met the Enemy and He Is Us"

This often-used quotation (Kelly, 1972) sums up the worldwide condition of capitalism and the ethical crisis of modern management. We are indeed our own worst enemies. We fight against ourselves by looking only to the financial aspects of business life and not its effect on the individual. We are too busy waging global economic warfare to worry about the human carnage on its battlefields. Business, for most of us, is a place where conflict gratifies greed rather than a source of energy for the improvement of mankind.

This is not surprising, as most of our experience has centered on campaigns in the undeclared war on communism. We have been constantly aware of the need to make our economic system "work" so that we could show the rest of the world that capitalism was a better choice. In this battle, we have loaned incredible amounts of money to third-world countries so that they could build their own versions of capitalism; we have rebuilt Japan and other Asian nations into nearly perfect copies of the American economic system; and we have openly shared the benefits of technology with all the world—including our communist competitors.

Over the years, we have lost many battles. But WE WON THE WAR! The evidence is in from such places as Korea, Taiwan, West Germany, and—the Soviet Union. Glasnost and perestroika are chapter and verse of the unconditional surrender of communism.

Why does victory pose an ethical dilemma? It's very simple. As victor, capitalism has inherited the earth and all its problems. There is no viable competing ideology to blame for economic and social ills. Capitalism and its managers are now totally accountable for the condition of business, government, and the quality of life of a rapidly growing fraction of the world's population. The burden of this responsibility is monstrous and can only be discharged if capitalism is made to "work" in near perfect form.

In this context, "perfect" capitalism is characterized by a free market where goods and services are judged by their quality and price; where interest groups have no control; where government acts to control abuse of economic power and to provide a safety net for those whose condition limits their access to opportunity.

When capitalism "works" in this form, it does a marvelous job of organizing production and services so that the quality of life of workers and consumers is significantly improved. When it doesn't, it can be as vicious as the most repressive totalitarian regime in which the majority fall victim to the greed of a tiny number of wealthy people.

We are now at a turning point in time when the concentration of wealth is such that it fuels speculation rather than production. In the stock exchanges of the world, speculation has resulted in grossly inflated prices that bear no relationship to the earning power of the companies whose certificates are traded. This is a worldwide problem and no capitalist system is immune. From 1982 to 1987, U.S. stocks increased in price by 250 percent. In Japan, the same period saw an increase of 600 percent; in Mexico, the increase was 900 percent (Batra, 1988). Even after major "swings" like that experienced in Japan, these markets remain grossly out of step with the underlying economic fundamentals.

But, isn't this okay? This is just another indicator of a healthy, competitive world market. No, it isn't okay. The underpinnings of sound money, growing productivity, and increasing employment are all missing. The result is a two-class world. A few very rich people, a shrinking middle class, and an exponentially increasing number of people living in poverty.

But don't we have nearly full employment in the United States? That takes care of poverty at home, doesn't it? No, it doesn't, and a couple of minutes with your pocket calculator will show you why. Suppose you are the sole wage earner for a family of four and that you want to live above the official poverty level of $14,335. Punch that number into your calculator. Now, suppose that you have a minimum-wage job—that's $4.25 an hour. Divide the $14,335 by $4.25 and you'll find that you would have to work 3,373 hours a year. That's 65 hours a week with no vacation or sick leave and you would still have to figure out how to support your family on $14,335. But, don't worry. You have a job and lots of company in America—about 37 million people.

You also have plenty of company worldwide. Nearly everyone in the world lives in poverty or at its edge. Hopelessness has never been as widespread as it is today. Even the United States has come under the sway of the imbalance between economics and opportunity. The 20 percent at the top of the United States income distribution earn about nine times as much as the 20 percent at the bottom. It's even worse in the developing nations: in Brazil the top 20 percent earns twenty-six—yes, twenty-six—times the income of the bottom 20 percent.

These income advantages have been obtained at the expense of our children's future. We have borrowed to excess for the present and ignored the reality of payment. We are the largest debtor in the world. Our balance of payments is always negative. And we have a growing underclass that has no hope of access to the benefits of capitalism.

We Have Met the Enemy and He Is Us

Yes, we are the enemy. We are rapidly turning the victory of capitalism into a major defeat. Through poor management and inept government, we are sowing the seeds of financial collapse and world rebellion. Make no mistake, if capitalism fails to deliver on the promise of a higher quality of life for those who live by it, politicians and managers will be the targets of justifiable rage.

These rebellions won't be simple demonstrations. In our rush to win the battle with communism, we have armed the world's poor. Military aid to third-world countries has created armed camps that make the National Rifle Association look like the St. Stephen's Ladies Aid Society. We have seen this clearly demonstrated around the world in places like Somalia and Bosnia, where armed bands wage full-scale wars that powerful nations are unable to stop.

We must not be fooled by the fact that most rebellions have occurred overseas. Every one of our cities is also a battlefield. Each teenage gang has more sophisticated automatic weapons than our local police. And, because they are the hopeless, homeless, and unemployable, they don't care if they get killed. They only want to get even with a system that has systematically and completely excluded them from any chance at a better life.

Many readers may be turned off by this negative scenario. However, it can't be sugar-coated to make it more palatable. These are real, immediate problems that take human form in social and economic statistics and in the issues they raise for the business community. Let's look at a few examples.

In the United States:

1. Poverty is on the increase. The decade of the eighties was a time when more young families with jobs fell below the poverty line. As usual, women and children were the ultimate victims. Today, one in three of our schoolchildren lives in poverty, and that number is increasing. As long as real wages continue their decline—currently those at the bottom of the income distribution earn only

about 85 percent of what they did in 1980—these statistics will continue to worsen.

- How can business create opportunity for young people?
- How can education and the other social services help these people to a better life?

2. The problem of poverty weighs especially heavily on minority groups. In the next fifteen years almost a third of the growth in America's work force will be made up of minority workers. Yet high school dropout rates, which hover at 25 percent nationally, are 50 to 60 percent among some minority populations.

- What will business do to secure the talent it needs?
- How can we train our citizens to compete in a global economy?

3. If these problems are not addressed, they breed despair and violence. In 1973, there were one hundred violent crimes per hour in the United States. Today, there are well over two hundred. Twenty percent of America's schoolchildren are armed, and they are using their weapons against one another and against the society that has fed their hopelessness.

- How are we to curb violence?
- When will we recognize the real threat of poverty to ourselves and our future?

There are countless problems like these facing us everywhere we turn. About 13 percent of United States adults are illiterate in English. There are 14 million children living in poverty in this country today. This is 17 percent of our children—against only 5 percent of the children in Sweden, 8 percent in West Germany, and 10 percent in Great Britain. More than half of the children in the United States live with just one parent—their mother. Few of these mothers received adequate prenatal care; their children suffer from birth defects; many have never seen a dentist, nor have they been immunized against preventable diseases; most have no access to proper housing; many are abused; and many are having children of their own.

- What are we going to do about these problems?

We have difficulty with these issues when they do not easily reduce to dollars and cents. When we are faced with untrained workers, we can readily count the costs of retraining. Or we compute the cost of firing them and recruiting replacements. What we cannot do is assess the human cost of their lack of skills. If we choose to fire the untrained, what impact will our decision have on their families?

From a global perspective:

1. The lack of opportunity in the third world continues to fuel a brushfire of migration. Boat people in southeast Asia, the dispossessed in the former Yugoslavia, and the northward-bound in Latin America are all subject to the push of misery and the pull of opportunity. Germany's experience with refugees tells it all. In 1980, Germany had no (that's right, 0) applications for asylum. In 1993, there were nearly a half-million such applications outstanding. Unless the opportunity gap between rich and poor people is closed, the developed nations will be inundated by waves of migration.

    - How can opportunity be homegrown?
    - How can the economically needy be separated from those who are persecuted?

2. As in the United States, despair leads to violence. Groups of disadvantaged people see themselves as victims of their competitors. Ethnic and national violence erupts and can no longer be curbed by superpower intervention. We see these forces at work in the transformation of the United Nations from a debating society to a police power.

    - How can global disputes be resolved without violence?
    - How are we to limit access to the means of violence?

3. People have found answers to many of these problems in a resurgence of religious and ethnic beliefs. The explosive growth of fundamentalism shows how powerful such forces can be and how they can submerge whole nations.

Consider: "The elemental fact that a majority of humankind on the face of the earth today is properly described as peasant and ex-peasant means that their responses to the harsh conditions of life they confront are sure to remain of capital importance. Insofar as their distresses find religious expression, fundamentalist movements . . . will continue to flourish throughout the foreseeable future" (McNeill, 1990, p. 563).

- What alternative beliefs can we offer these people?
- How can the fundamentalist be drawn into our business and political systems?

The implications of these alarming trends for business leaders lie in the fact that all of the above problems are driven by a simple relationship.

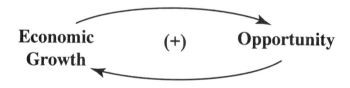

As economies expand, they create opportunity which, in turn, feeds further growth. That's all there is to it. When people have opportunity, they can raise themselves out of poverty and cool the anger that drives fundamentalism, migration, and violence. Opportunity also makes it possible for nations to invest in the future and especially in young people so that the economic engine can continue to deliver on the promise of opportunity.

Solving the Problem

Just knowing about the opportunity crisis is a major step in the right direction. However, there are no simples "fixes" for the problems described above. Although we believe the solutions lie in ethical action, no ethics course or corporate code of conduct will ensure our success. Neither will an ailing democratic capitalism direct the energy and resources to the real needs of people. Nor will outdated views of economic systems grounded in the "invisible hand," "monetarism," or "trickle-down" theories be effective in guiding the actions of the global business leader.

We need, instead, a *new ethical paradigm* which can help us link actions to consequences. This must be a paradigm that puts social justice in first place. Yet it must not be so unrealistic that it fails to catch the interest of business women and men. This agenda must bring together the moral imperatives of a world culture, the power of dominant economic systems, and the self-interest of the individual business man or woman. If it cannot do so, the statistics of misery will increase and we will have ensured the failure of democratic capitalism.

The Parable of the Commandments

There was, in those days, a trader of great prowess whose decisions were the envy of Wall Street. This was Norah. At the counting house where she worked, she was much sought after. Many went to her for advice as to specific trades and for discussions of her views of the market at large.

None was more solicitous of her advice than Bradlee, who had recently come to the house from a place called Ivy League. Bradlee was imbued with the Spirit of Ivy, which taught that all was measured by gain and that each trade should be weighed in the balance of cost and earnings.

When Bradlee and Norah spoke, they would often come to cross purposes where Bradlee's standard of gain would confront Norah's view of the common good of investors, employees, and consumers.

There came a time when Norah noted that her conversations with Bradlee were becoming tests of her thinking. "Your principles would not bring an investor as great a gain as would be the case should he or she use my standard."

While she could still show Bradlee the way to benefit all, Norah saw that these questions required long discourse to answer. Many were the times she lamented the lack of a set of guiding principles which could be the rock on which ethical trading could be built. In vain, she searched ancient and modern texts. Fruitless were her consultations with the management gurus, who seemed to know not of what they spoke.

It came to pass one day that she wandered to the roof of the New York Stock Exchange during her nooning. There, she leaded on the parapet and looked across Wall Street and the coming and going of traders.

She watched them as they gestured to one another and she could imagine how each was recounting the gains of the morning. She murmured to herself, "If only there were other principles to measure the work of a morning. How much easier it would be to do what is right for all who are touched by this economic system."

Her thoughts were apparently unheard.

Then, lo, there seemed to appear to her a set of ethical commandments—a new paradigm—full-formed in her mind. General principles whereby ethical behavior might be fostered within the frameworks set by business.

She was amazed, for it seemed to her that a Voice had spoken. One that was clear and immediate. Yet she remained alone on the roof.

She puzzled on this for but a moment. Then she went from the roof to her own counting house where she crafted the Commandments on her word processor, secure in the knowledge that they represented a higher level of principle than that much in use on Wall Street.

The Ten Commandments of Doing Ethics in Business

I. TALK THE TALK OF SOCIAL JUSTICE.

II. WALK THE WALK OF SOCIAL ACTION.

III. PUT PEOPLE ON THE BOTTOM LINE OF CORPORATE CALCULATION.

IV. DO RIGHT YOURSELF, DON'T LEAVE IT TO GOD.

V. DO WHAT IS ETHICAL, AND YOU WILL DO GOOD BUSINESS.

VI. LET YOUR WORK INTEGRATE FAITH AND FINANCE.

VII. CAST ASIDE THE SYMBOLS OF INDIVIDUALITY AND DEFINE YOURSELF BY THE CONSEQUENCES OF YOUR ACTION.

VIII. RECOGNIZE THAT ECONOMY, OPPORTUNITY, AND SOCIAL JUSTICE ARE THE LEGS ON WHICH WORLD SOCIETY STANDS.

IX. GIVE THE EXTRAVAGANT GIFT OF YOUR COMMITMENT TO SOCIAL JUSTICE.

X. REMEMBER: PEACE AND PROSPERITY IN ALL THE WORLD ARE CREATED BY ETHICAL BUSINESS PRACTICE.

CHAPTER 2

Talking the Talk: Social Justice

The Parable of Price

In the autumn of the year, Norah would go into her garden and take from a tree standing there an apple. This she would take to Wall Street so that she might eat it when trading ceased for the day. One day, as she cut her apple, her assistant Bradlee came into her office.

"Norah, might I sit with thee? Let us eat our lunch and review the trades of the day."

"Surely Bradlee," she replied, "I see that you have a banana for yourself. Come, let us sit here by the window."

When they were seated, Bradlee pointed to Norah's apple and laughed. "Norah, why is it that you work all the summer to raise those few apples when you could more cheaply buy such a banana as this?"

Norah finished cutting the apple and asked, "Is the banana really so cheap?"

"Oh yes; for only one small coin, I am able to enjoy this remarkable fruit."

"Why is that so? I would think that a banana would be very expensive, for is it not transported from afar?"

"Verily, that is so. But our government does subsidize the trade in bananas so that its market price is always very low."

As Bradlee peeled his fruit, Norah asked, "But someone must pay for the subsidy. Who does that?"

Bradlee frowned. "Surely that is obvious, Norah. Sometimes you amaze me with your ignorance of trade. The government pays, of course."

"And who is that?" she asked.

"Why . . . just the government," he answered.

"Bradlee, it is you who are ignorant. When the government pays, it is every citizen who must be taxed. Thus, every person, rich and poor alike, has paid for your banana. Whereas, my apple is the fruit of my labor and I have paid its full cost."

Bradlee considered this and said, "But without the subsidy, I could not afford to eat bananas. And I don't like apples."

Norah laughed. "Bradlee, that is the essence of the truly free market. You may choose what you wish, but only if its price reflects the full cost of its production."

"Consider this lesson," she continued, "true prices tell us all we need to know about the things of life. They speak of the costs of materials and labor and they show to us what it is that the people wish. If we fail to give price freedom to speak, we can conceal corruption and injustice."

Bradlee finished his fruit and gazed from the window for a time. Then, thinking to confound Norah, he said, "What you say is all very well for bananas. But what of today's trades? Were not all stocks up? Did not record volumes pass through our trading arena? And were not the prices of stocks determined by the new tax laws announced yesterday? How does your lesson fare with these realities?" He sat back, smiling at his victory.

She then taught him, saying, "It is my lesson writ large. The prices you saw today were lies. They did not tell us of value, nor did they measure the earnings of the companies that issued them. Instead, they spoke of speculation and greed. Were not the stocks bought by those who hoped to gain by speculative bidding?"

Now humbled, Bradlee answered, "Yes. But that is the nature of the market."

"Verily," Norah said, "a market corrupted by governmental interference and speculation. And I say to you, if we do not banish these from our trading arenas, our system of value will collapse. If price is allowed to lie to us, we must be prepared to eat of the fruits of its deception."

In Search of a New Ethical Paradigm

The manager of the nineties is adrift on a sea of talk. There are endless waves of new words that express the uncertainty of global business. Often the whole language of management changes to accommodate a new set of practices that take us all by storm. We are in search of a new way of thinking about business—a new approach to management—and we are writing the language that we will use to talk about where we are going and how we will get there.

We can find abundant evidence of the turbulence in management by returning to our airport bookstalls and looking more closely at what managers are writing and reading. The waves of new words are lapping onto the covers of books telling managers about Total Quality Management, Just In Time Production, Learning Organizations, and Strategic Planning. These ideas are presented as sound bites that can (it is assumed) be mastered in one minute or less. Managers are being told, in effect, that the old ways of doing business are no longer useful and that success requires a new way of thinking and talking about business.

When taken together, the ideas presented in the typical bookstall have a more profound message. There is a qualitative movement away from our traditional approaches to management. Not too long ago, popular books looked very much like a watered-down version of the typical MBA curriculum. Operations, finance, personnel, and marketing were the key words in the titles of the books in yesterday's collection. When we compare these words to those we see today, it is clear that management thinking has shifted from *concrete* to *abstract*. For instance, Total Quality Management is an *abstract* idea—a set of very general management principles that do not specify how Total Quality is to be attained. In contrast, traditional approaches to Quality Control were *concrete:* application of standard statistical techniques would enable managers to measure Quality and guarantee that Quality standards would be met.

Why is this happening? Why do management writers and increasing numbers of practitioners look at their work in a new light? The simple answer is that the world is changing and traditional management no longer works. The more complete answer is that *accelerating* change is calling for a comprehensive overhaul of management—new practices, new perspectives, and a new language.

Management as a Second Language: In Search of a Paradigm

In the past two decades, world business activity has come to resemble the capitalist paradigm. Organizations operating under this paradigm are owned by shareholders, managed to realize a profit, and continually forced to respond to the demands of customers and the marketing efforts of competitors. At the same time, these organizations are increasingly subject to global competition and to the movement of capital to areas where return is greatest. These developments have created the emerging version of management—an international second language spoken by business men and women in virtually every country.

Management as a second language is most obvious in those countries formerly a part of the Soviet Union. There, the communist paradigm is being overthrown in favor of a new capitalist paradigm and managers are expected to master the "second language" in short order. First, and foremost, these managers must transform state-owned organizations into privately-held companies.

Thus *privatization* is the foundation stone of the "second language" now being learned by managers in eastern Europe. We can see how this single concept leads to a whole new language by considering its linguistic foundation. As *privatization* has moved to center stage for this new generation of managers, they have been forced to set virtually every problem in the dialect of financial management. Informed administrators are expected to know the marginal cost and revenue associated with each product or service as well as the interest of the marketplace in their offerings. Consequently, *privatization* is defined by a number of conditions that must hold in the organization.

Similar changes in the "second language" of management are going on across the world as managers attempt to make sense of their environment. Quality and competitive advantage define the market and service builds the loyalty of customers. The modern manager is a student of the business environment—continually seeking to shape the interaction between the organization and its surroundings.

The Social Consequences of Business

Just adopting the old business paradigm is not enough. We can already see that Western institutions and practices do not flourish when transplanted into the newly free soil of emerging nations. The mixed success of the traditional business paradigm in these environments is due to its inability to deliver the social consequences people expect. Market economies have led to increasing poverty, privatization has resulted in ownership by old elites, production pipelines remain filled with poorly made, unwanted goods, and, most of all, there is a crisis of opportunity.

A Capitalist Manifesto

The new business paradigm is one that must take root in traditional capitalism. People across the globe see capitalism as the only viable economic system, and, more significant, it is welded in place by the fact that the second language of business is spoken in every nation. This new paradigm cannot, however, be a simple restatement of old capitalist principles. It must come to grips with the fact that the moral issues of social justice are what will determine business success and the ultimate survival of a reformed capitalism. Money, morality, and power are the key words to be learned by speakers of the second language of business.

Money and power have always gone hand in hand in traditional capitalism. For the successful capitalist, Money Is Power; power to shape business organizations and power to influence governments. Morality has rarely been of much concern in the practice of capitalism. The result has been *accelerating* growth in social injustice and polarization of the world's people into the haves and the have-nots.

In a new Capitalist Paradigm, the people on the short end of the global quality-of-life scale must be at the center of our concern for social justice. If these individuals are to gain access to food, health, education, and opportunity, there must be a pragmatic definition of justice that can guide the decisions of those who control money and power. Simply put, money and power must not be so concentrated that people are victimized by their use.

The link between social justice and economics is nowhere more obvious than in the major cities of the United States. There whole communities have joined an underclass in which poverty and violence go hand in hand. These are communities whose residents cannot escape without major changes in the economic systems that have created them in the first place. Such changes cannot occur unless Money, Morality, and Power come together in business decisions.

If we are to achieve social justice at home and on a worldwide scale, we must understand the integrative force of this triad of spheres or systems. They cannot be compartmentalized as separate and distinct aspects of reality without great loss of effect. When any one of these three is isolated from the others and its perspective is the sole guide to action, we have a breakdown of social organization and a rise in social injustice.

Economists, for example, often do not appreciate the dynamics of politics and religion as these affect the distribution of wealth, the division of labor, or the means of production. They are in as precarious a position as the politicians who ignore economics and/or religious values. Similarly, the religious leader who fails to understand economics or politics can do little to shape these systems to the principles of social justice.

The Capitalist Manifesto: Can capitalism as we know it today provide the social and economic structure that can integrate Money, Morality, and Power? The answer is a qualified "yes." Capitalism can do the job, but only if it puts its house in order and brings its considerable energy to bear on the social injustices it has helped to create.

It must become *democratic capitalism*—business at work for all the people, controlled by the people. Its agenda is not a narrow definition of profit, but a broad concern for social justice and the quality of life of employees, stakeholders, and citizens.

The reason that social justice has been such a difficult problem for the capitalist is that it has been defined out of our thinking about business. On the other hand, communism was particularly appealing to most of the world because it had put social justice at its center. It is not hard to see why the door of the third world turned to communism when its most visible promise was a better life. Contrast that with capitalism's promise of hard work and rewards down the road.

If we are to make capitalism work on a world scale, we need a Capitalist Manifesto that defines a set of values on which business and social systems can be built. The cornerstone of this manifesto must be social justice. From a purely pragmatic view, the sheer numbers of the disadvantaged compel us to make improvement of their condition the primary objective of our activities. Then the democratic aspects of capitalism can function to an end that has wide appeal and the potential to enlist the commitment of all individuals.

The central mechanism in democratic capitalism is freedom. Unlike communism, in which the state controls the economy, capitalism emphasizes choice in a market controlled by price and quality. When this works, as it has to some extent in the United States, human liberty has flourished as never before. Government has been excluded from control over business. However, it has defined an environment where individual freedom is guaranteed. As these systems have worked together, they have given more access to quality living to a greater fraction of the people than any other economic system in the history of man. As Irving Kristol has stated: "Never in human history has one seen a society of political liberty that was not based on a free economic system, i.e., a system based on private property, where normal economic activity consisted of commercial transactions between consenting adults. Never, never, never. No exceptions" (in Prodhoretz, 1982, p. 99).

Under a democratic capitalist system, people have an equal opportunity to pursue their own goals. Such people can, without oppressing minorities, influence social development by freely exercising their political and moral persuasions. Given time, conviction, and stamina, these people can effectively correct abuses and social injustices.

Freedom is not, however, license. When democratic capitalism provides the framework for individual initiative, it is writing a social contract. Thus, when the state protects individual rights, it does so in the larger interest so that such general goals as the "pursuit of happiness" can be achieved.

As new problems arise, the social contract changes to include new obligations for all of us. Business, as one of the primary beneficiaries of governmental protection, must also accept its share of these obligations. When it does so, in the open environment of democratic capitalism, it makes its power available for correcting social and environmental problems beyond the scope of individual action.

When we speak of democratic capitalism, we are referring to open access to a free, honest market. A place where price does not lie. Where the flow of trade corrects rather than creates social injustice. Above all, democratic capitalism functions best when it is controlled by persons whose behavior is open and honest. Ethical conduct in a free market is the essence of democratic capitalism. It is also an ethic that recognizes the responsibilities of the social contract. By working within the spirit—as well as the letter—of the rules, business can further the social goals of government. Only in this way can the "democracy" of capitalism be assured to all who live under its dominion.

We can see how honest "talk" works in the Parable of Price, where Norah shows that the market itself must "talk the talk" honestly and openly if it is to be the foundation on which we can build opportunity. In this parable, price is only an example—it is social justice that business leaders must "talk."

THE FIRST COMMANDMENT

Talk the talk of social justice

CHAPTER 3

The Parable of Ethical Action

From time to time, the nations of the world would gather to conduct games of grace and skill. These games would test the speed, strength, and control of men and women of all races and creeds.

There was, at one of these games, a runner of surpassing power, one who would always lead his opponents to the finish line. His success raised a suspicion among the governors of the games so that they tested his body to see what might account for his many victories. When they found that he had made use of a forbidden potion, they stripped him of his medallion and banished him from the games.

When this news reached Wall Street, Bradlee rushed in to Norah.

"Norah," he said, "have you heard that the mighty runner, Benjamin, was found to have taken the forbidden potion?"

"Yes, I have heard this. Is it not dismaying?"

"Terribly so," he agreed. "Benjamin will lose much gold and silver. His value to business is much diminished."

"That is not what I meant. His action strikes at the very foundations of the games. For are they not to be tests of men and women against one another, without potion or advantage?"

At this Bradlee laughed and said, "Norah, you are not of this world! Any athlete who would win at these games must make use of any means. The shame of Benjamin is that he was caught."

Norah was astounded. But she did not cry out. Instead, she sought to teach Bradlee the consequences of unethical behavior.

"Bradlee, have you seen the new offering of stocks? Here it is written that New Ventures is trading at an all-time low. Surely you should purchase this stock for your own portfolio. I, Norah, so advise you."

Bradlee, knowing of Norah's prowess, gave her the use of much of his wealth to purchase the New Ventures for him.

Not many days had passed when Bradlee again rushed into Norah's office.

"Norah! Have you seen? New Ventures has failed! My wealth is much diminished!"

"This I know, Bradlee. As I knew that it must fail."

"Oh, Norah," he cried, "this you cannot do! You have tricked me and caused me to trade my wealth for worthless paper. It is not ethical!"

Norah then smiled. "You have reasoned correctly, Bradlee. But suppose that this knowledge were hidden from you. You would be saddened over the loss of your wealth, but you would attach no blame to me."

At this, Bradlee stalked about the room. "Before God, Norah, you are wrong! It was wrong to conceal your knowledge! I trusted in you and you betrayed me!"

"Oh, Bradlee. Let your faith be strengthened. I seek but to teach you the lesson of ethical action. See, here is your wealth. It is not wasted, merely held by me for a time."

He rejoiced at his good fortune. But he was troubled at Norah's deception.

"Why, Norah, did you trick me?"

"To show you that there is only one right course of action before God. To act fairly and ethically is the precondition for all interactions of men and women. It is not enough to escape detection, for that is the way of evil."

At this, Bradlee was much disturbed. "But, Norah, how shall I know what is right in the beholding of God?"

She chided him, saying, "Think, Bradlee, on your investments. You took issue with me when I kept information from you. I took advantage of you."

"Yea, that is so," he agreed.

"Then, let that be your guide. Take no advantage of another. And, remember, even if no man can behold your acts, God sees you and will set your actions right in his own time."

Bradlee was much puzzled at this. "But, Norah, how will I know when I have done right? Could you not set down for me a set of rules so that I would know what to do?"

Norah smiled. "No, Bradlee, you know within you what is right. Your intuition is the best set of rules there is. When you ask yourself 'Am I doing right?' as you make your trades and give your advice, you will be using the intuition the Lord God has given you. And, you will do no wrong to others."

Walking the Walk

Following the First Commandment, talk the talk of social justice, has not been particularly difficult. Politicians have consistently used social justice as the key that unlocks the door to office. They have continued to voice platitudes about access, equity, and opportunity while doing little or nothing to make these concepts a reality for their constituents. Business leaders have been no less able to talk the talk. We have become accustomed to hearing corporate executives extolling the social conscience of their organizations while their objective actions foster pollution, price fixing, and shoddy quality. It's easy to talk the talk.

Walking the walk of ethical action is much more difficult. Those who would walk this walk must force their way against a pretty substantial crowd moving in the other direction. Their ethical actions will constitute real risks as they call business and politics as usual into question. They will also be lonely advocates of business and political practices that make for real social justice.

As new generations of business leaders set out on this walk, they will need a sense of direction that can provide the support and energy required to buck the system. Direction comes, we believe, from within each of us. We have an intuitive grasp of ethical action and the capacity to evaluate our own behavior. What many of us lack is the sense of shared purpose that can turn our lonely walk into a triumphal march.

Monasteries on Wall Street?

An earlier draft of this manuscript carried the title *Monasteries on Wall Street* (DeThomasis, 1988). That title was chosen as a metaphor whereby business leaders could see the consequences of their action from a different perspective. The metaphor still retains its shock value and draws our attention to the morality of business life. To be sure, it is a catchy title; but the metaphor is more subtle and powerful. Monastic life has something to say to modern business, a timeless message that can be especially relevant and useful as we set out on our walk.

The Wall Street monastery gives us a way of thinking about the relationship between business and society. It is a new metaphor that shakes up our traditional thinking about the world of commerce so that we can see our problems in a new way. Such metaphors are powerful guides to thought and behavior. They determine how we will use money, knowledge, and power; how we will judge proper action; and the pathways our organizations will take in the future.

The monastic metaphor we are proposing for Wall Street is based on three features of traditional religious life:

- Groups of people, set apart from society, working together to attain social justice

- Members of these groups who have made specific commitments to shared goals

- A common code of action to which each member subscribes

Chapter 3: The Parable of Ethical Action

These principles have served to govern monastic life from the beginning of recorded history. Every religious movement—Eastern or Western—has captured its essential energy in the collective commitment of those who chose to live the monastic life. In the past, these people took special pains to give up secular life, often choosing vows of poverty, chastity, and obedience. If this is what we mean by the monastic paradigm, we can't expect to enlist many new members on Wall Street!

But we don't want our Wall Street monks to be poor; we want them to work for the eradication of poverty. We can't expect them to be chaste, but we can insist that they be honest in their personal lives. Above all, we can't demand obedience; we seek, instead, freedom that is guided by ethical values. In short, we are looking for that sense of purpose which can empower those who would walk the walk.

With this definition in mind, let's see how our paradigm might look in a Wall Street monastery.

Collective action and common goals: Those of us who work on Wall Street already act in groups. We attempt to solve the problems of modern finance so that our company and its clients prosper. Often we work in monastic cells—called "workstations"—where we use the mysteries of Lotus 1-2-3 to illuminate the spreadsheet manuscripts of trade. In many ways, we are already monks. What is missing in our collective work is a clear sense of shared purpose that rises above profit. As Norah has told us, price (and profit) are essential to our work. However, how we get our profits and what we do with them is not a part of our current paradigm.

The monastic metaphor is one in which social justice is the goal toward which profit is directed. Modern monks work at the computer and in meetings to maximize profit. As this is happening, they are constantly concerned with the human consequences of profit. Has it resulted from the production of quality products? Has it produced more good jobs? Has it helped to achieve a greater measure of social justice? With this common orientation, there is plenty of evidence that we have a foundation for a monastic movement on Wall Street.

But, it is practical? And, can the new monasticism survive in a materialistic environment? Maybe . . . It will depend upon the emotional strength of those who walk the walk and their ability to excite others to follow in the path toward social justice. Taking the first steps on the walk is witness to others that there is a serious new movement afoot in the business world—one that can enlist converts and empower them to overturn the unethical.

Making commitments: Taking the vows listed above is not a matter of forsaking the world for life in a Wall Street monastery. Rather, it is the integration of business life with the world outside. This is where our monastic metaphor diverges rather sharply from traditional religious life. Where the classic monk was disconnected from the secular world, our modern counterpart takes action to use money and power to moral ends.

Walking this walk involves taking new kinds of business risks. Walkers continually seek profits that are intimately bound up with social justice. These "monks" care about the welfare of people and society and act in a way that produces both profit and social results.

A few years back, *The Wall Street Journal* quoted a speaker who spoke indignantly about "the unfair advantage children of affluent, stable families have over children raised in poverty. He urged a massive new transfer program designed to take money from the prosperous and use it for the benefit of the poor. . . . He scolded his largely well-to-do audience: Society can only work when we are willing to share with one another" (30 May 1985).

This sermon was not delivered by some liberation theologian or pastor with Marxist bent. The preacher was none other than one of the most widely known right-wing free-enterprisers in the world, H. Ross Perot. In the same speech, Perot went on to note that "community and risk sharing" were attributes of a business life with social consciousness. A compelling foundation for vows that we all should be taking.

A common code of ethical action: The rules of traditional monastic life dealt with work, social interaction, and prayer. These were specific and coercive and led to daily patterns of life that did not vary appreciably over the centuries. Obviously, we could not write a set of specific rules for ethical conduct in business that would hold up for more than a few days. When we have tried to set down these rules, we have produced a kind of "ethical joke book."

Chapter 3: The Parable of Ethical Action

What guides our modern monk is not a set of rules, but a firm intuition of what is right. We all have an inherent understanding of what is good and right. Businesspeople have a capacity for moral reason; an innate ability to make oral evaluations; and the persistence to see their actions through to improve the human condition. By building on an intuitive sense of what is right, the Wall Street monastery does not need to be caught up in religious debate. It can get right down to work on the problems of the day and see to it that the advantages inherent in our capitalist system are never unfairly taken. If we wait for the rules to be written, we will be forever prohibited from making ethical decisions. Most of us on Wall Street already know what is "right," we only have to let our intuition have its sway over our daily actions.

THE SECOND COMMANDMENT

Walk the walk of ethical action

CHAPTER 4

The Parable of Corporate Justice

Norah's time was that of the great rationalization. Men and women had come to know a sufficiency of their affairs to be able to predict the course of events with great accuracy. Using computing engines, they were able to craft complex models of their organizations and finances that could easily reveal the future consequences of present action.

Bradlee was among the most highly skilled of those who practiced rational thought. His nimble fingers could devise arrays of numbers—called spreadsheets—that embodied all that was essential in business life.

One day, when Norah was walking among the cubicles of those she supervised, she came upon Bradlee, intent on his work.

"Forsooth, Bradlee," she said, "you seem near wedded to thy computer. What is the nature of its charm?"

Bradlee started at her question. "Norah, you frightened me! Here I am working with the latest release of 1-2-3. It is of singular beauty, is it not?"

"That I could not say. What does it show thee that gives it such appeal?"

"Just this. I have devised a model of the operations of General Toaster Corporation. See! At this keystroke, I can calculate the internal rate of return!" At this, he pressed (F9) and the screen flicked to exhibit new values.

Norah examined these carefully. As a jest, she said, "These look very much like the entrails of the secretary of the treasury."

Bradlee was offended. "For shame, Norah. This is a serious matter. Here I have proved that a cut in wages can make General Toaster much profit."

"How is that?" she asked.

"Why, look. In AA56 we see that General spends $1,500,000 in wages. If I put this amount to ten percent, it increases IRR to twenty-six percent. Is that not impressive?"

"Verily," Norah agreed. "But how is that cut achieved?"

"Easily. General is a nonunion shop, so it can reduce hourly wages to the rational minimum. Surely you can understand that!"

"I do so very well," she replied. "Each worker at General will take less money home. Is that not so?"

"You have it! See how easy it is to plan for profit using 1-2-3?"

Norah considered this, saying, "What of the workers? Would they rejoice and praise your model?" Bradlee stared at his CRT and turned to Norah with a frown. "Norah, why ask you this? The workers do not count in the equations of profit. If they had worked more diligently in the past, they would be making more money now."

"What you say is true, Bradlee. But who is at fault? Is it not so that the managers at General have made many bad decisions? Have they not failed to modernize their plants? Have they not ignored many suggestions made by their workers?"

"Exactly!" Bradlee was thrilled that Norah had finally grasped the essence of his model. "My model erases these errors. By investing in new plant and curtailing wages, General can rise from its ashes. Why, my model . . ."

Norah did not let him further praise his work. Instead she said, "Bradlee, your model is faulty. It does not include the human equation. Here, let me show you."

She then sat before his console and began to shape his model to human ends. First, she added a calculation of worker productivity. Then, she arranged the incantations of the model so that higher wages resulted in higher productivity. Finally, she distributed a portion of the gains realized by productivity to the workers.

When she had finished, she turned to Bradlee. "Now run your model. Let us see how General fares under these conditions."

Bradlee did as she asked. As the model progressed through successive quarters, productivity, wages, and profits grew continually. Seeing this, Bradlee was at once critical of Norah.

"Oh, Norah. You have created a loop of logic in the model. Productivity leads to profits, which fuel wages, thereby further increasing productivity. Your model has the sin of circularity."

"No, Bradlee. It has the virtue of compassion. It shows how the condition of workers is necessary to the strength of the company. What you call circularity is the most fundamental human condition. Productivity and reward cannot be separated."

Thinking on this, Bradlee said, "But how will I convince the managers at General to accept these principles? They are exceedingly greedy and narrow-minded."

"What you say is true," Norah replied. "You must use the power of your model to show them that the compassion hidden in its equations will provide gains for all. Remember that those who eat of the Lotus are easily transported into a dreamworld where ordinary concerns cannot penetrate."

Social Justice: A Corporate Report

If we are going to establish a new paradigm in the business community, we need to know our starting point. We need a "corporate report" on the condition of social justice in the business world. Such a report will give us a sense of the changes that will have to be made in corporate life in order to achieve our goal of social justice. Let's examine where we are in a language we can understand, that of assets and liabilities.

Social justice—assets: Ethical action has played an important role in the success of many companies. When we link ethical practices to the bottom line, we have clear evidence that "ethics works." Corporations that have focused on ethical behavior have greatly improved their relationships with customers and the general public. They hold a secure position in the market and are usually more profitable than those companies who pay no particular attention to ethics.

In a similar way, the concern for quality in products and services brought about by Japanese competition has worked wonders in many companies. This theme has been played out again and again in American corporations. Those companies delivering high-quality products and services at reasonable cost are both sought after and profitable. They also happen to be places that offer a quality work life to their employees.

These tangible results have lent support to a growing concern for ethical behavior in the business community. In a recent survey of accredited business schools, the Ethics Resource Center discovered that 92 percent of the schools included ethics in their curricula. In addition, there has been a proliferation of short courses, workshops, and retreats in which ethical topics are discussed. These developments go to show that there is a growth in our ethical assets; we are able to report that our concern for ethics has increased and that this has resulted in stronger companies and a better bottom line on our balance sheet.

Have these ethical gains been translated into social justice? Have ordinary people benefited from the ethical actions of business leaders? These are more difficult questions as they go to the outcomes of corporate activities. They can best be answered by looking to those who evaluate the corporate conscience for the purpose of investment.

The example we offer is the set of policies followed by the Christian Brothers Investment Services, Inc., which we include in an Appendix to this book. From this perspective, socially responsible action involves: a) Research and Dialogue with corporations to determine how their products and services impact people throughout the world; b) Education to alert business men and women to socially responsible policies and practices; and c) Ownership Actions to influence corporate policy.

These approaches are targeted by CBIS on several general ethical issues. *Labor dignity and equality* promotes affirmative action, equal employment opportunity, comparable-worth wages, safety, and the fair use of transnational labor. *International justice* centers on human rights and the relationship between economic development and individual opportunity. *Militarism* avoids support of the weapons industry and is sensitive to those corporations attempting to convert from defense to commercial activities. *Environment* recognizes the impact of economic life on global life systems and seeks to support those corporations who act to conserve resources and avoid pollution. *Bioethics* addresses the emerging link between human life and the corporation and encourages those organizations dedicated to improvement of the human condition.

What makes these values important to business leaders is that they work! CBIS has been a markedly successful service that consistently outperforms its competition. In addition, it has had a direct effect on the policies of many companies by exercising stock voting rights. Its history shows that it is possible to *put people on the bottom line.*

Social justice—liabilities: And it works the other way, too. Between 1977 and 1982, Beech-Nut engaged in systematic adulterating of its infant apple juice product, even going so far as to transport the adulteration operation to Puerto Rico to escape regulation. The result? A two-million-dollar federal fine and a reduction of market share from 19.1 percent to 15.8 percent (Kindel, 1989). Unethical behavior also works in the marketplace—and it reduces the bottom line to create ethical liabilities.

Our experience with legal problems in recent years has led to the adoption of codes of conduct in many of our corporations. In a study of these codes at 02 Fortune 500 companies, researchers found that matters of honesty and legal compliance were emphasized in more than 75 percent of the organizations. However, it was also discovered that such concerns as product quality, civic affairs, and personal character were not mentioned in 75 percent of the codes reviewed. We have decided to do what is legal, but we have not yet committed to some of the more fundamental ethical principles.

In fact, some of our best-known corporations permit (if not encourage) behavior that is obviously unethical. Tobacco companies have targeted much of their advertising at young people—

Joe Camel has been held responsible for major increases in adolescent smoking. These same companies have also expanded into the third world where there are no governmental restraints on tobacco products and the deadly consequences of their use can be hidden behind a smokescreen of advertising.

In our financial communities, we find some of the most flagrant violations of codes of ethical conduct. Insider trading and junk bond machinations are but the tip of the iceberg of manipulative behavior. Studies of trading pits in stock exchanges have found that each pit encloses a "culture," which may be more or less ethical. Some of these financial "cultures" exist only to prey on investors to turn their assets into commissions for traders without regard to the standards of fair play.

In our liability accounts, people come up "in the red"—they take a distant second place to profit. This is nowhere more obvious than in the "downsizing" of the American corporation. The monstrous layoffs in the computer industry are cases in point. These inhuman actions are taken to conceal management blunders so that the short-term financial statements paint positive pictures. Consider the case of Control Data Corporation. In the early 1980s CDC was one of the major players in the mainframe computer market. However, it failed to enter the game of personal computing and neglected to redesign its product mix. Consequently, CDC became an outsider to the explosive growth of the personal computing industry and a much weakened combatant in the mainframe market. At this writing, there is no longer a Control Data Corporation—it is now several small, weak businesses whose survival is questionable.

The CDC case is notable in that its demise can be laid at the doorstep of management. Management is responsible for the thousands who lost their jobs—people who were unqualified to compete for another job in a market they did not understand. Despite the failure of these managers, they were able to leave the wreckage of CDC with multimillion-dollar severance benefits. People weren't in the accounting equation that divided up the company and distributed the spoils.

Social justice—net worth: The bottom line of our statement of social justice liabilities is that we will do what is necessary to comply with the law. But we will rarely take steps to improve the conditions of work for our employees or the benefits of quality for our customers—to say nothing of social justice. It is a statement with a considerable amount of "red ink" as to the effect of business on people.

The evidence cited above leads to the conclusion that we have been "eating our ethical seed corn" for some time. We have used up the capital of confidence held by our workers and customers and are in danger of losing any sense of shared values. This is critically important to the future of our businesses. We cannot function when our customers are unable to believe in our advertisements; when our workers cannot commit themselves to our organizations; when the things we make and the services we provide lead to ever greater social injustices.

An ethical business plan: Despite these negative numbers, there is hope for improvement of our ethical condition. We can take measures to create a corporate environment where ethical behavior is emphasized; where ethics take precedence over short-run profitability. Our business plan is based on the following general principles:

1. The ethical environment: This is a corporate culture that is based on a shared sense of mission and stewardship; a culture in which responsibility and accountability are founded on basic ethical principles. In this culture, everyone Talks the Talk of Social Justice.

2. Ethical actions: We recognize that business is carried out by making decisions and choices. In order to do this ethically, we need to take the interests of others into account and trace the impact of our decisions on employees, consumers, and the general public. In effect, we plan our activities in an ethical context in which the results of our actions are subject to continued scrutiny; we Walk the Walk of Social Action.

3. Values and codes of conduct: Our business plan emphasizes the critical importance of shared values and mission. It does not attempt to control behavior by codes of conduct. Rather, it puts processes and procedures in place that cause us to examine ethical issues in all aspects of

our business. In this way, ethics become a bottom line in and of themselves; they tell us how people are affected by our business activities.

4. The corporate conscience: We also include those who have an interest in the decision-making process. By involving stakeholders, consumers, and directors in the planning of corporate activities, we ensure a hearing for those who might be affected by our actions. These make up a "corporate conscience," which recognizes that the corporation is a living entity that must be held accountable for its actions.

5. Funding the plan: We also know that ethical conduct must be supported. The plan must originate from inside our organizations, and it will require time and money to make ethical behavior a reality. Beginning with a corporate commitment to social justice, we plan to build ethical considerations into all aspects of our normal business practices.

But let us be very clear on one point. Ethical business plans must be business plans. They must be founded on corporate strength and profitability—else they will fail. The surprising discovery is that such plans can be made and viable corporations built on the integration of people and profit.

A case in point is the Fastenol Corporation of Winona, Minnesota. This manufacturer of "nuts and bolts" has been growing at an annual rate of 30 to 40 percent for the past ten years. Its president, Robert Kierlin, collects an annual salary of $120,000 with no increase in the past five years. Instead, the benefits of Fastenol's growth are shared with employees. With people on the bottom line, there appears to be no limit to the success of this company.

Accepting and acting in accord with the social justice paradigm takes on concrete form as we put people on the bottom line. Technology and the numbers it generates are not the ends of business—they are the means whereby business can deliver on its potential for social justice. This puts people on the bottom line of any corporate report and makes them an integral part of the equations of daily business life.

THE THIRD COMMANDMENT

Put people on the bottom line of corporate calculation

CHAPTER 5

The Parable of Technology

There was sent out in those days, from the Valley of Silicon, a calculating engine of awesome power and speed. This engine went through the land like a plague of locusts. No home or hamlet was safe from its insidious influence until the whole nation was dependent upon it. This was the computer, and Wall Street, too, was among its most avid users.

Each scribe on the Street had a device in his/her cell whereby communications with the computer might take place. Calculations without end were performed and reports without number were produced.

Norah saw these things. They seemed to be good. But her heart was troubled. Why did not the concerns and needs of people emerge from these data?

One day it came to pass that her assistant, Bradlee, came into her chambers. He said, "Norah, on this pleasant day, I would that we journey forth into the countryside in my new BMW chariot."

Norah knew that this was good and they left the City in high spirits. As they journeyed up the Vale of the Hudson, Bradlee extolled the merits of the computer.

"Norah, did you know that we now have a number for each person who trades with us? And, with that number, we can direct all the financial transactions the client may wish to make?"

Norah thought on this and said, "But Bradlee, is it not possible that we have lost touch with the human being who carries that number?"

"Nonsense!" he replied. "For is it not written that the Lord God watches over the fall of each sparrow?"

"Verily, that is true. But the Lord God does not fly for the sparrow. Neither does he decide the direction and time of flight. He only watches the fall and considers it in the scheme of nature."

At this Bradlee laughed. "Norah, if the Lord had a computer, he could program all sparrows so that none might fall."

"Then, Bradlee, there would be no sparrow. Only a made thing. And there would be no joy of flight. Remember the Lord God exalts in freedom and randomness. Only in the larger order of things does his wisdom shine forth."

At this, Bradlee was silent. He reflected on what Norah had said and was troubled.

Later that day, they reached the ancient city of Troy. There Bradlee said to Norah, "It is said that there is a new computer of surpassing power in the citadel of learning called RPI. Would you see it?"

Norah agreed and they went to the place called RPI. There they were told that the computer was resident in a disused chapel near the center of campus. At this, Norah was alarmed. How could a computer be made compatible with the house of God?

They entered therein and were met by an acolyte. He conducted them into the crypt where reposed the CPU. It was attended by many other acolytes, cleaning, adjusting, and adoring.

Upon seeing this, Norah asked, "How is it that many must serve the computer? Is it not a tool of mankind?"

The acolyte was puzzled. "Verily it is a tool of mankind. But many must serve it else it goeth down. Then all learning at RPI must needs stop."

Norah was amazed. "Is learning, too, dependent upon the computer? I have always thought that learning was a gift of God to each person who might use that gift according to their ability."

Chapter 5: The Parable of Technology

The acolyte scoffed, "That is an old-fashioned idea. Why, today, learning cannot take place without the computer. Come, let me show you."

He conducted them to the main floor of the chapel. There pews had been replaced by individual desks where earnest scribes stared at CRTs. The altar had been removed and a priest was ministering to the computer through a complex console. Above their heads, the choir loft was populated by systems analysts.

Beholding all this, Norah was exceedingly angry. She went forthwith to the altar and cast the priest aside. With a single gesture at the console, she caused the CPU to go down before her. Then she taught them, saying:

"Oh ye misguided! Cannot you see that you have become slaves to the machine? Is it not obvious to you that you see only that which the machine chooses to reveal? Do you not realize that you are but a number in its convoluted calculations?"

The scribes and systems analysts were angry at Norah's questions. They said, "Begone, woman! You know nothing of these things! This is a world of numbers and information and we are masters of it."

"Silence!" Norah said. "This is God's world! And no person is a number. Each has God-given rights and abilities which must be given their full play in all human intercourse. I ask you, could the computer you worship be created in a world where no person was free to think, and decide, and succeed or fail on the merits of his/her action?"

They heard and were ashamed. They knew that they had set up a false god and that they had let their god gain control over their human condition.

They praised Norah and conducted her out of the chapel to a grove of trees, where they all gave thanks to God for revealing the error of a life in which numbers failed to speak of people and social justice.

God, Why Me?

A sound ethical business plan isn't enough. Ethics in business depends on the individual. Each manager and each employee must make a commitment to shape their behavior to ethical standards if the plan is to succeed.

We have spent a good deal of time making the case for social justice. We have shown the practical value of ethical conduct for business as a whole. Despite these arguments, the proof of ethical value is still in the hands of the individual. Corporations cannot contribute to social justice unless managers and employees take personal responsibility for their actions. And it is appropriate to ask, "God, why me?" For to be ethical, each of us must break with the ruling paradigm of profit.

Taking the risk of being ethical: Business is by its nature a game of advantage. If we know more than our competitors, we are likely to be more successful. If we have a greater stock of capital than another investor, we are likely to become richer. If we have the larger market share, we are likely to dominate our competition and, in the long run, merge them into our corporation.

To be ethical, we must give up some of this advantage. We must report some of our secret information, share the earning power of our capital, foster competition. These are very real risks that are necessary first steps in making a commitment to ethical behavior. This does not mean that we have to give away the store in order to be ethical. It does mean that we must be continually sensitive to our advantages and how we use them. In a truly democratic capitalism, business is changed from a zero-sum game to a fair contest in which all parties stand to benefit. The risk we take is that of opening up the game to a new set of rules that stress a commitment to social justice, an openness of process, and a focus on results. These justify the risks.

Earning and sharing: We can't insist on individual commitment to ethical action without dealing with money. It remains a powerful measure of the individual and the principal reward for risk taking. To a great extent, our success in ethical development will depend on how we use money and motivation for gain. Remember that money, morality, and power are the keywords of ethical talk.

In capitalist thought, we have tended to separate money and morality. This has probably done more to create our current ethical problems than all the abuses of insider trading, price fixing, and product quality taken together. Religious organizations are not immune to the separation of money and morality. By reason of their universal influence and material resources, many churches are among the most powerful institutions in the world today. The power to harness the spiritual and material dimensions of humanity as well as the imagination of its members in an integrated way makes religion potentially the most awesome of forces. However, instead of having a healthy understanding and appreciation for such power, churches propose to be "modest and humble." They feel uneasy with their wealth. Instead of introducing modern management techniques and making themselves more open and public, they are forced into secrecy in their decision making because they simply cannot admit to themselves, much less to the public, that wealth is good if managed properly and for the benefit of the people.

Contrast this point of view with the perspective of Pope John Paul II, who told entrepreneurs a decade ago, "The degree of well-being that society enjoys today would have been impossible without the dynamic figure of the entrepreneur. Without any doubt, your services are of the first order for society." Thus the power of economic activity is beginning to be united to the spiritual mission of the church to bring the benefits of economic activity to all people. Money, morality, and power are becoming key terms in the language of the church and religious men and women are beginning to "talk the talk."

The same argument works at the individual level. Enjoying one's personal income and wealth is dangerous only when it is hidden and not used also for the benefit of people. When it builds through speculation and is withdrawn from productive investment, it weighs on economy and society. Thus, ethical capitalists are free to make and to enjoy money—but they are also charged to use it to the benefit of employees, customers, and the general public. This has been the traditional strength of the "Jewish Economic Man," whose considerable business prowess has always had a strong social conscience (Tamari, 1987).

By way of example, we can turn again to our pocket calculator to find out how much money you should make. Take the lowest annual income you would be content with as a basis for your career—and make it well above the official poverty line. Now, multiply that number by the number of employees whose jobs depend directly on you. The result is a measure of your worth and a ballpark figure for your income. The point is, you can make all you want—if you take care to provide attractive jobs to those who work for you, and you use your wealth to foster social justice among those who are touched by your business activity.

A good illustration of this point is found in a recent article by George Wilder, in which he examines the *Forbes* report on the four hundred richest people in America (1988). He argues that most of the very rich do not wallow in their assets; instead they put them to work to build ever-stronger corporations and to extend their business concepts to more customers. He states, "Wealth to the businessperson is what freedom of speech and access to the public are to a writer or to a politician. It is the businessperson's very means of production. . . . Wealth to the wealthy is their entrepreneurial knowledge and commitment. It's the resources to continue expanding successful enterprises without first gaining the approval of remote boards of experts, politicians, or bureaucrats" (p. 349). From this point of view, wealth is the power to act. To do good—or evil. Therefore, the question as to how much you should make is rather, "What am I doing with the money?" If your resources are a measure of the good you and your organization are doing, then let them increase without limit. Wealth enables you to "walk the walk"—but you must take the first steps on your own.

God, why me?: Because you are called to the life of a business community whose fundamental objective is social justice. Each decision you make, each action you take does not exist in a vacuum; it serves the purposes of your organization and contributes to the distribution of justice. There is no such thing as valueless action. To imagine that your business activities are neutral is self-deception. Wall Street must be peopled by you and others who have chosen to act ethically, who have accepted the risks and responsibilities. Yours are the rewards of income and power that come about through the widespread acceptance of the

Social Justice paradigm and the Ten Commandments of Doing Ethics in business.

Let God's Fingers Do the Walking

Throughout the history of capitalism, the "walk" taken by business leaders is one that has trodden upon others in the rush to profit. It is a "walk" that has been accelerated by the use of knowledge and technology to increase money and enhance power—with no concern for the morality of its pathways. Today, capitalism is no longer "walking"—it is "running" to keep pace with an explosion of technology.

No matter how impressive our technology, it must always be weighed against the impact it has on ourselves and others. When technology is the sole driving force propelling business, it produces side effects of monstrous proportions. It endangers workers, pollutes environments, and makes business and social decisions—often without human intervention. For the democratic capitalist, the issues raised by technology require that business walk a fine line between technological costs and benefits. We cannot leave to God the responsibility to join together what technology has put asunder.

As we look back over decisions made by governments and businesses, there is pretty conclusive evidence that we have "let God's fingers do the walking." There has been a sort of "divine determinism" which we have given free rein over the social and environmental consequences of action. In earlier times, this translated into a noninterference pact between man and his environment.

There is a story in Spanish history that illustrates the roots of this "Yellow Pages" view of God. During the reign of Philip II, someone suggested that two impassable rivers, the Tajo and the Manzanares, be made navigable in order to rid the area of poverty. The government commissar exclaimed, so the story goes, "No! If God so willed that those rivers should be navigable, then He would have made them so with a single word!" In other words, God's fingers were to direct the larger social and economic issues of the times.

Contrast this proposal with government policies in Brazil, which have decreed the building of roads through hitherto impassable jungle—again, in order to improve the lot of the impoverished and to promote economic development. That these same roads lead to deforestation, erosion, and desertification is of little concern to the decision makers. They have let God's fingers walk over the ruin.

If only God would clean up the social and environmental mess we have created. What bliss humankind would enjoy if God alone would work in history. All we would need to do then is conduct business as usual and let God's fingers do the walking—in search of solutions to the problems of the times.

Despite our tendencies to rely on God as mechanic, we know better. We know only too well that there are those who make things happen, those who watch things happen, and those who wonder what happened. Contemporary business leaders—no matter what their faith or lack thereof, no matter what their economic bias, no matter what their management style—know that modern-day financial networks coupled with sophisticated technology and human insight can control the destiny of humankind. They know that they must be counted among those who make things happen. We can no longer ask why God permits evil, poverty, and oppression to exist in the world. The power to create our future is with us here and now. It is our fingers that must do the walking.

As we flip through the technological Yellow Pages, we must balance the science of the possible against the human consequences of action. Technology is indeed a "strange god" who must be approached with care. Technology, alone, cannot meet the social needs of the times. It is the *power* within the troika—with *money* and *morality* it can shift the benefit-cost equations of management in the direction of social justice. But only if it is shaped to human ends.

This requires the integration of managerial power with the real world of personal and social tragedy. It also demands the same integration of values and economics from the humanist. Without integration, the inevitable result is compounded social injustice, poverty, famine, and war.

Integrating Money, Morality, and Power

The critical importance of the integration of economic power and social concern is evident in the growing worldwide emphasis on human rights. This is a melding of three very distinct political views of "rights." Western societies champion the rights of the individual over the state. Marxist polities take the converse position of the right of the state over the individual. The third-world nations probably see this balance more clearly when they demand the rights of self-development and self-determination.

Social justice results when these perspectives are in balance—when the state facilitates individual freedom and when that freedom is used to enhance the self-determination of others. To say that these ends can be achieved without attention to economic issues is ludicrous. Marxist blindness to the individual makes a travesty of freedom. Capitalist inattention to the consequences of economic decisions wrecks social and biological environments. Deistic appeals to God are empty of action.

These readily observable results show that the business-value integration must be at the center of our social justice paradigm. We must master technology and shape it to human ends. If we fail to balance its very real power with a concern for human consequences, we have set up a false god that can destroy human identity.

This means that the gulf that exists between religious and business value systems must be bridged, possibly by a mutual understanding and respect of technology. As any careful assessment of paradigms shows, there is a division of labor that gives business control over technology and religion control over values. If this division persists, there is little hope that technology will be mastered; it will remain godlike and wait upon God to correct its mistakes.

Our dependency upon technology was greatly increased in the decade of the eighties, when computing became a part of all aspects of our lives. At work, our activities are shaped by computers; at home, we are entertained by them; the affairs of the church are managed by computers; and countless instruments of daily life are shaped by computers. We have truly given computing dominion over much of our lives and have accorded software a godlike status that lets that god walk our walk for us.

THE FOURTH COMMANDMENT

Do right yourself, don't leave it to God

CHAPTER 6

The Parable of the Junk Bonds: Doing Ethics in Business

In the acquisitive society of those days, money changers were continually adding to their wealth by speculating in corporate stocks. The value of these documents would rise and fall in great measure and the clever investor could realize great gain in their trade.

Norah saw all this and was alarmed. Rarely was the value of a stock determined by the true worth of the company of issue. Instead, values were set by speculators and soothsayers who divined forthcoming mergers and acquisitions. These activities were especially troubling to Norah when her house became involved in the manipulation of value. As was often the case, Bradlee gave form to her dilemma.

"Norah," he said, "I have great news for you. I have now spoken with Slim Pickins, the giant of the leveraged buyout."

"Now, that is interesting," she replied. "Why should he seek your counsel?"

Bradlee laughed. "Oh, Norah, he has no need of me to tell him what to do."

"I thought as much. What then is the good news you bring?"

"He would give us leave to work with him on a takeover of Super Foods! Think of that! The largest grocer in the land! Why, the stock would surely triple in value . . ."

Norah held up her hand. "Bradlee, hold a moment! How would Pickins carry out this scheme? Even he hath not the means to purchase a controlling interest in Super Foods."

"That's what I've been trying to tell you, Norah. We would issue bonds leveraged against some of his assets. Their sale would provide the financing for the takeover. Isn't that a keen stroke of business?"

"It is indeed a stroke," she said. "But, is it ethical? Are not these junk bonds, as their face amount would needs be much greater than Pickins's worth?"

"Norah, Norah." Bradlee sighed. "When the takeover is finished, Pickins will be worth double. Then the bonds are not junk—they become instruments of worth."

"Verily. But what of the deception? And what of those who hold Super Foods stock? Will not speculators buy their investments and will not they lose in the takeover?"

"That is so. But what of it? The trading of stock is fraught with risk."

Norah saw what Bradlee did not. She then cast the scales from his eyes.

"Bradlee, junk bonds were not named in vain. They seek to hide reality. They are, by their very nature, unethical."

"But Norah, that is the idle talk of priests and scribes. Surely you cannot let such opinions shape what we do."

"Bradlee, my friend. Ethics is what we do. Think on this. What of the accounts you manage that hold Super Foods stock. What advice will you give their owners?"

"That is easy. I will tell them to sell to Pickins."

"Tell me then. Will he not sell off Burgerland? Will he not close Saltridge Farms and sell their lands?"

"Surely! That is but good business, and my stockholders will profit greatly."

"And will the employees of Burgerland similarly profit?"

"Well . . . no. A new owner needs to reduce staff . . ."

"What of the migrant workers who now are employed by Saltridge Farms? Where will they work when the land is sold to developers?"

"Why, I suppose . . . Norah, why do you this to me? It is not my lot to protect these workers. If I were to do so, there would be no speculation and . . ."

Norah interrupted. "Now you see ethics in action, Bradlee. When we speculate, we distort value and jeopardize the livelihood of workers. We play our investors false: for as surely as they have gained by takeover, so shall they lose by divestiture."

Doing Ethics in Business

Ethics and action are the "odd couple" in modern business. Business leaders govern their actions by the principles of growth and gain—leaving ethics to churches and advocacy groups. This is the natural result of an ethic that has been intellectualized, debated, and emasculated of purpose. Ethical concerns have become matters of belief and ideology—light years removed from the decisions of the marketplace.

The thesis of this book—that ethical behavior is the means to social justice—is an attempt to focus ethics on the transcending principle of the condition of all men, whether capitalist, Marxist, or simple revolutionaries. Too often ministers, CEOs, and so-called liberation advocates package their beliefs as ethics. These are forced on others without benefit of actions as a reference point. It is as if ethics in action is forging ahead with its own principles of growth in power and gain in numbers of believers—leaving business to pursue similar ends with no realization of how these goals *must* be related.

There is another side to this argument. Ideology can be so powerful as to control the actions of business men and women. A business ethic that is manipulated to fit ideology will not work; it will consume those who use it and those it affects. But the sermons of the ethical ideologue are hard to resist. They are cast in learned terms, seeming to build logical structures that are compelling guides to our thinking. This is a corruption of thought.

As William McGurn has noted, ideology is to philosophy as gluttony is to fine dining (1985). He goes on to make the point that ethics as ideology detracts from the human condition and does not enrich it. The ethical ideologist is a "hatchet man" who shapes people, organizations, and society to his or her needs: "What has made the ideologue so deadly is that like Procrustes he cuts people to fit his idea, not vice versa. Hence Auschwitz, hence the Gulag. . . . Neither science nor religion has ever demanded nearly the faith that ideology does" (McGurn, 1985).

Ethics as ideology is irrelevant and threatening to social justice. If ethics is to be relevant in the modern world, it must produce real results that define its underlying principles. In other words, business leaders cannot give lip service to ethical principles—they must put these principles to the test of action. And be prepared to be judged in terms of the results. The power that business leaders possess is the instrument for doing ethics in business. In our social justice paradigm, ethics is not ideology, nor is it politics. It is action. More important, in democratic capitalism, ethics is *business action.*

This is the central strong point of the new paradigm. It replaces symbols and discussion with action. In choosing the title for this chapter, we chose to borrow from Donald Jones to say that we should "do ethics in business" and stop talking about it. In rejecting the ideologies of the past, Jones recognizes that they fail modern managers as they face the complex issues of the times.

"In this changed business environment the traditional ethic with its outdated assumptions was no longer able to identify and answer the major new ethical questions that the modern manager faced: questions of market power, oligopoly competition, pollution, the quality of working life, occupational health, race relations, affirmative action, foreign bribery, consumer safety and welfare, privacy, weapons production, corporate governance, disclosure, organizational politics, conflicts of interest" (1982, p. 138).

This list of issues gives business leaders an ethical agenda of sufficient scope to occupy their energies. They need not waste their time defending the American free enterprise system. That can be left to the academics. The ultimate defense of capitalism is not found in the arguments of intellectuals. It is written clearly

Chapter 6: The Parable of the Junk Bonds

in the human consequences of the actions of manufacturing, service, and financial organizations. Where we "walk the walk" of social action, we are linking ethics and business with the result that *both* people and business will profit.

What is the evidence for this statement? Haven't there been countless examples of the profitability of unethical practices? We must admit that the recent history of capitalism is not overly rich with examples of rewards for ethical action. Instead, monstrous profits have been made by those who have flaunted ethics. These, however, are short-term gains for which our society as a whole pays dearly. A couple of examples show how high the price can be.

When the savings and loan industry was deregulated in the early eighties, there was a rush to expand the business of these institutions. As competition increased, ever more risky loans were made—many to the directors and managers of the lending organizations. When the inevitable occurred, and the thrifts failed, these loans were written off and the money pocketed by those entrusted with its management. Their personal gain is yet to be priced, and the public will be saddled with tens of billions of dollars in costs.

Deal-making of this kind varies from the unethical to the clearly illegal. In the BCCI scandal, depositors were bilked and drug lords enriched through the manipulation of banking laws. The American legal advisers of BCCI have made millions of dollars in direct fees and countless additional millions through sweetheart stock deals. None of these profits will be returned to the depositors, none of these lawyers will go to jail. Instead, the legal system will grind away for years while those who engaged in unethical conduct will be free to enjoy their gains.

The costs and benefits of unethical conduct are not always as obvious as these examples suggest. Sometimes, unethical behavior can cut away the foundations of the social system. When members of political systems become snarled in the net of corruption, they not only profit—they destroy the foundations of the systems they are elected to protect. Congressional leaders who take advantage of their position to get, and act upon, inside information are making strictly legal profits. At the same time, they are putting themselves in positions where political actions can lead to further profits. The result is a weakening of public trust and the nurturing of contempt for ethical and legal behavior.

In these examples, personal, short-term gain is purchased by public, long-term cost. Clearly, there is a downside to unethical action. This conclusion brings us back to the original question, "Can *both* business and people profit by ethical behavior?" This is a complex question that has at least three levels of application. First, does ethical conduct lead to good business in the large? Second, if corporations engage in ethical behavior, do they remain competitive and profitable? Finally, if we as individual business women and men act ethically, do we advance in our organizations and share in its rewards? Let's consider these one at a time.

During the past two decades, there has been an increasing concern as to the impact of business on people and social systems. These interests first emerged as colleges and universities began to question their investment policies. They not only divested themselves of involvement in pariah states like South Africa—they also created policies whereby the practices of corporations could be judged on ethical grounds. The net result of these activities takes the form of a number of "social choice" accounts in which investment dollars are targeted on those organizations that make a positive contribution to social justice. Does it work? You bet it does! In its most recent report, the College Retirement Equities Fund Social Choice Account showed an annualized three-year return of 13.3 percent—a full percentage point above comparable alternatives.

Okay, so investors can realize the benefits of ethical actions taken by corporations. What about the companies themselves? Recently, the CEO of Johnson and Johnson surveyed fifteen companies that had written, visible commitments to service. These companies averaged an 11 percent compounded growth rate over thirty years. This is three times the growth rate of the GNP in the same time period. Investment in ethics has truly paid off for these companies. There is, however, a caution in our conclusion. To make ethics work for the corporation requires a long view of business activity. Ethics won't show up on the bottom line in the next quarter—or even the next year. It is a way of behaving, a commitment to customers, a kind of social conscience that takes time to communicate. The corporations that have the insight and the will to wait it out will be far stronger than their competitors.

The same set of risks plays out at the individual level. Ethical managers will have to take the longer view of their careers—and be willing to sacrifice some of the immediate payoffs that go to those who give low priority to ethical action and social justice. In the longer run, the ethical manager will benefit, as has the ethical company. The growing importance of ethics in major companies is testimony to this point. At this writing, 20 percent of major American corporations have a position for an "ethics officer"—a person whose whole career is bound up with the issues we are raising in this book.

In the Parable of the Junk Bonds, we once again show the downside of unethical action. Unfortunately, it's necessary to dwell on the negative as the ruling business paradigm does not ask the kinds of questions Norah puts to Bradlee in the parable. For those individuals and companies willing to ask these hard questions, there are long-term, durable gains to be made. Ethics is good business.

THE FIFTH COMMANDMENT

Do what is ethical, and you will do good business

CHAPTER 7

The Parable of Stewardship: Faith and Finance

The great religions and temples of those days were much concerned with money. Famous priests reached out to their congregations with the power of television to add contributions to mountains of treasure. Others invested the donations of believers in speculative ventures of questionable merit. Still others gathered riches around themselves so that they were as the princes of old, living in splendor on the widow's mite.

Norah was appalled at these excesses. They were, for her, very personal. For the resources of the churches were very much a factor in the markets on Wall Street.

Bradlee was much taken with one of these priests. By managing the investments of the Church of the Word, he had come to know its leader, Dr. Hardsell, and to appreciate his message.

One day, as Norah walked among her people, she saw Bradlee busy at his terminal. He was so intent on his work that Norah was able to watch him for some time before she was noticed.

Finally, she said, "Bradlee, those are trades of great scope. Who is it that has such a large account with us?"

"Oh, Norah. I did not hear you come. This? These are the trades of the Church of the Word. Are they not large?"

"Indeed. That is what I noticed. But what funds are these? How is it that the church has these vast resources?"

"Surely you have heard of Dr. Hardsell. None is more skilled at evangelism."

"If, by evangelism, you mean collecting money from those of modest means, I would agree. But does not Dr. Hardsell promise that donations will be used to further the work of the church?"

Bradlee laughed. "Surely he does, Norah. But he is cleverly investing in the market to multiply these gifts. Is not this what Christ himself did in feeding the multitude?"

Norah frowned. "Bradlee, Christ used his power to multiply the loaves and fishes for the good of many. I cannot see the actions of Dr. Hardsell in the image of Christ."

"Oh, but they are very much the same. Don't you see? Dr. Hardsell is using the power of the market to serve many with but little means."

Norah responded, "Is this not the same Dr. Hardsell whose mansion lies far out on the Long Island? Is he not the same who has created the Lord's Playground?"

"Verily. Only last week I visited him at the Playground. Why, it is more extensive and merrier than Six Flags Over Texas. The roller coaster was made in Switzerland and covers more than . . ."

"Cease!" Norah said. "Bradlee, how can these perversions be linked to the work of the Lord? Where in this fairyland are the poor in spirit? Where are the hungry?"

"Why . . . none needs go hungry. There are stands where all may seek nourishment at every turn. And the games uplift the spirits of all who attend."

"Bradlee, I speak not of the simple pleasures of an afternoon. What of the fundamental needs of those who live in misery? How will the antics of Dr. Hardsell change their lives in any meaningful way?"

Bradlee thought on this. "Well, I suppose that . . . maybe the church will . . . " He stopped and frowned.

Chapter 7: The Parable of Stewardship

"You see, Bradlee, Dr. Hardsell cannot pass the simple test of stewardship. He collects and multiplies resources for his personal gain. He has created a false empire cloaked in righteousness with its foundations in greed."

"But Norah—even so, isn't he just doing good business?"

"That least of all! He has fouled business as well as religion. He uses business to manipulate people to his own ends. Never does he seek to use its power to achieve the ends that his church professes."

"Then he must needs be a false prophet!" Bradlee exclaimed. "Let us throw over his account!"

"No," Norah counseled, "let us instead use the wealth he has taken from others to invest in those activities that will do good. There are yet securities that will give good return by doing what is right for workers and consumers. Let Dr. Hardsell help these companies with his money."

"I can see that you are right, Norah. But how can I prevent what he is doing at the Playground?"

"This you cannot do. But you can use every opportunity to counsel him to use its profits to the benefit of others. Perhaps you can show him how virtue can live with value. Remember, when faith and finance are separated, they feed on each other to build perversions, and never do they then do good."

Bradlee considered this and said, "Verily. But Dr. Hardsell will receive what I say and reply to me with an obscure biblical reference. I cannot debate him."

"Then just read to him from the Rule of Saint Benedict on stewardship. For it is written, 'As cellarer (or steward) of the monastery, there should be chosen from the community someone who is wise, mature in conduct, temperate, not an excessive eater, not proud, excitable, offensive, dilatory or wasteful, but God-fearing, and like a father to the whole community. He will take care of everything . . . . Let him keep to his orders.'"

"Excellent, Norah! These are all the qualities lacking in Dr. Hardsell. If they are pointed out to his followers, perhaps some will take up the question of stewardship."

"Let us hope so," she replied, "for there is a sickness on the land whereby greed has replaced stewardship. And it cannot be cured unless each of us shows the faith we have in the humanity of everyone."

Faith and Finance

The behavior of Dr. Hardsell is, alas, all too common in the confused ideological environment of today. The unfortunate mixture of religion and money created by televangelists illustrates how the values underlying ideology can be perverted, as well as the power of ideology in shaping behavior. Even in this extreme, ideology helps many explain the world and assists the few in exploiting it for their own personal ends. However much we may be dissatisfied with these approaches, we cannot change our need to explain the world in broad terms. This means that new points of view and labels will have to be found to guide our thinking about the ethics of business. Especially if we are to deal with the ethical questions of the type facing Bradlee and Norah.

We have already begun this work by choosing a social justice paradigm to explain the condition and behavior of business leaders. This is, however, not sufficient; we not only need to integrate our beliefs—we must be sure that our values are translated into actions. In the social justice paradigm, we have the seed of an integration of faith and finance.

Much of the trouble we have experienced with failed ideologies comes from our blind faith in their pictures of man and society. When Marxism deifies the state, it forces the individual into an amorphous mass whose collective good is a justification for personal misery. When capitalism promotes competition, it fails to recognize the relative advantages of the competitors and allows misery to grow within prosperity. Faith, in these ideologies, has been misplaced. It has shaped our allegiance to abstractions that are far removed from concerns for social justice and individual freedom. If we are to avoid the errors of our failed ideologies, we must find a place for faith—a place where it can inform business and social life on a daily basis.

For most of our history, faith and finance have been at opposite poles of human concern. On one side of the polarity are those people of "faith" who care about what happens to humanity; on the other side are people of "finance" who care just as much about what happens to employees and customers. These concerns are not as far apart as they seem. Faith and finance are two dimensions of the reality we call society. Whenever we separate these perspectives, we are likely to fall into the traps set by simple ideology.

Bernard Murchland has described the separation of humanism and business in the United States: "We are still a country of two cultures, one of higher things and one of practical affairs. High culture is commandeered by an intellectual elite; commerce is regarded as of a lower order, an intruder in culture's house of sweetness and light. This narrow notion of humanism creates in America the special problem of cutting off large areas of experience from a humanizing influence" (1984, p. 45).

The dichotomy of faith and finance is, however, basic to Western thought. It is firmly rooted in philosophical polarities such as spiritual versus material, sacred versus secular, religious versus worldly. It is also very much a part of the belief systems that govern daily life: nature versus technology, mind versus matter, knowledge versus wisdom. Given the deep-rootedness of the faith-finance division, we cannot expect that it will be easy to bring them together.

In fact, almost every aspect of our economic and cultural life is, to some extent, perverted by an imbalance between faith and finance. Consider the charitable organization that pays its executives inordinate sums of money—money that clearly fails to serve the purposes of the organization. For example, the CEO of the Memorial Sloan Kettering Cancer Center has an annual compensation of over $700,000, and the president of New York University receives benefits of nearly a half-million dollars. The president of the United States makes a good deal less than these leaders—about $200,000. In the face of these numbers, we have every right to ask: Is it faith or finance that is driving their efforts?

Bridging the Gap

The social justice paradigm offers an alternative in which faith and finance become one through ethical behavior. By acting always to achieve social justice, we must, necessarily, include both values and resources in our daily decision making. The strength of this approach lies in the fact that our survival as a species in a global environment requires ethical behavior. Narrow self-interest and strident nationalism cannot suffice when social and biological systems are at risk.

The emerging concern for ethics in business and government is a signal that our paradigm is "on target." Mankind—in the form of world society—is in the midst of a search for a higher consciousness. Increasing numbers of people have experienced an uprooting of comfortable and familiar cultures; dogmatic facts have been invalidated by new discoveries; standard operating procedures no longer work; and new paradigms of thought are replacing the outmoded beliefs of the past.

This is fertile ground where the seeds of faith and finance can be sown. The ethical behavior that unites these resources is, however, a fragile plant. It must be nurtured by the daily actions of all people, who must exhibit their concern for mankind in what they say and do. Most important of all, the unity of faith, finance, and ethics must not be allowed to find a comfortable home inside our failed ideologies. If that should happen, global problems would be explained away in familiar terms and social justice would be assigned to God so that we can carry out business as usual.

One need only look to the chaos in the former Soviet republics to see what little power there is in failed ideologies. When perestroika was initially proposed, Soviet leaders assumed that small changes in the communist paradigm would promote social and economic development. Instead, the ideology of communism failed catastrophically, and people looked to capitalism for solutions to everyday problems.

The example applies to the integration of faith and finance we are proposing in that the fact of ethical options makes our old business ideologies useless. Once the failed paradigm is rejected, there must be a new alternative—we cannot return to our old ways. We are required to find a new paradigm that will validate our global condition and will enable us to use faith and finance to power the management of our social and physical environments.

Faith and Finance: A Personal Matter

The dilemma facing each of us can be seen as one in which the ideology of social justice confronts the prevailing ideology of gain. We are often unable to cut through the dilemma to action. Only when we employ our considerable skills to shape rather than confront ideology are we able to make the transition from ideology to action.

Ideologies have failed mankind in general. But they have also failed each of us in a very personal way. They have encouraged us to place our faith in large-scale systems that grind individuality into some amorphous grist for unknown purpose. We come, in time, to worship these ideologies and their attendant systems and let them control us.

Alan Storkey has captured the surrender of our autonomy in the following passage:

> That which people worship becomes their master. Gradually over the decades the economy, and its special form of knowledge, have been granted autonomy. Faith has been vested in the market, the power of money, economic progress, patterns of manipulation and the automative benefits of materialism. Economists who have declared themselves pure and unstained by any faith have been tacitly bowing down to these masters. The idols have failed. We have bowed down before the idols we have made and now they laugh at us. How silly to worship markets when they are our handwork. How pathetic to treat the state as some kind of magical solution. How vain to vest in bits of paper which have created the control of our economic policy (1986, p. 62).

We have seen how faith in ideology clothed in objective, scientific principles leads only to confusion in our thinking. Unfortunately, misplaced faith also leads to paralysis of action in the everyday world of business. Each of us feels powerless to effect meaningful change in our economic system and in the ways that system shapes our business activities. This is the ultimate deception of ideology: diminishment of persons, faith, and individuality.

Ethically oriented business leaders must throw over the limitations of ideology and integrate faith and finance in their own actions. They must dare to act and to believe that what they do will make a difference. This is by far the most difficult step in becoming an ethical manager. The scope of the problems we face, the resistance of our organizations to change, the pervasiveness of greed all contribute to our feelings of helplessness. It is very tempting to find yet another ideology and place our faith in its workings so that we can float on the economic tides of the times.

The case against surrender is quite clear. We don't have the time to drift. Instead, we need to roll over and start swimming against the tide of injustice. To do this, we will need to see our world in a wider perspective where economic, social, psychological, and yes even (especially) spiritual life becomes part of an integrated whole that can give us courage and purpose to act as committed individuals.

The context of human misery gives an urgency to our need to integrate faith and finance, to use the power of economics as the means to address the problems of humanity and its environment. Because these problems are immediate and their consequences critical to the survival of humanity, there can be no time lost in integrating faith and finance.

By recognizing the unity demanded in the Sixth Commandment, we can liberate the power of faith and finance in ways that can benefit everyone who holds a stake in our economic systems.

THE SIXTH COMMANDMENT

Let your work integrate faith and finance

CHAPTER 8

The Parable of Individuality: One Body

The society in which Norah lived was not a community. It was a loose grouping of individuals. Each person strove to make him or herself unique. They robed themselves in gaudy colors, each trying to exceed the other in cost or cut of garment. All took great pleasure in his/her possessions, lavishing great care on their chariots, decorating their abodes at great expense, and ensuring the utmost of comfort for themselves. No thought was taken for others among these people.

Nowhere was the cult of individuality more assiduously practiced than on Wall Street. And no more ardent practitioner existed than Bradlee. His was the most splendid abode; his the chariot of greatest prowess; his the robes of most brilliant color. These things Norah observed. They worried her greatly, for, by practicing individuality, Bradlee was growing ever more distant from his work and his community.

As Norah watched these signs, it came to pass that she began to notice a change in Bradlee. He no longer arrayed himself in splendid colors; he talked less of his abode and more of his work; and he was less eager to be gone to evening and weekend pleasures. Norah noted these things and wondered at them.

One day she had need to visit another counting house and had no means of transport. Calling upon Bradlee, she asked, "Bradlee, would you convey me to the other end of the Street, as I have no chariot at my disposal?"

"Oh, Norah. Woe is me that I cannot grant thy wish."

"But why, Bradlee. Is not thy BMW chariot, called by thee 'Kaiser Bill,' in fine fettle?"

"Alas, Norah. I have sold Kaiser Bill to another. I am bound to use only public transport."

"But Bradlee—surely this is a strange decision. You placed much pride in Kaiser Bill. How could you part with such a possession?"

"It is indeed strange, Norah. But I came to see that I had no need of such an expensive chariot. It was but an indulgence of little consequence."

"That may be," she answered. "The funds you received from its sale could be profitably invested elsewhere."

At this, Bradlee seemed embarrassed and turned to his work, wishing to end their conversation.

Norah, however, was quick to notice his discomfort. "Come, Bradlee, what is it that you do not say? How have you used the proceeds from the sale of Kaiser Bill?"

"Norah, I am loath to tell thee that I did not invest in a wise venture. Instead, I joined my funds with those of two others like myself to finance a housing cooperative in Brooklyn."

Norah was amazed. "Why, Bradlee, this seems like a very worthwhile project. How works the venture?"

At her interest, Bradlee became animated. "Why, Norah, we can purchase and repair two apartment buildings. These we sell to poor tenants at very low interest rates. We take care to school them in their care so that their value increases. It has given me much pleasure to see these needy people find quality housing in which they can invest their modest means."

On hearing this, Norah reached across Bradlee's desk and took his hands. "Bradlee, you have accomplished much by this action. You have turned from looking inward at yourself. You have become part of the community and its problems. Moreover, you have taken the riches formerly lavished on yourself and put them to good use."

Bradlee smiled. "Yes, Norah. I saw that personal indulgence was depriving others. Strangely enough, I value myself more than I did when I was defined only by my possessions."

Norah smiled into his eyes. "You have learned that we are all members of one body and that our strength lies in our solidarity with one another. When we walk alone in the light shed by the glitter of our possessions, we are stumbling into darkness. When we follow the path shown by the radiance of our concern for one another, we are marching toward justice and fulfillment."

The Cult of Individualism

The greatest threat to the attainment of social justice in our time is our hedonistic worship of individuality. Each of us is truly an island, existing apart from every other and defined in symbols rather than substance. We *are* our personalized license plate or our designer jeans. We wear our headphones everywhere and receive much greater quantities of communication than we give.

As we have come to know Bradlee, we have seen him as the complete individual. All of his skill and energy has been directed at improving his own life. Only by intervening in fairly dramatic ways has Norah been able to shape his thought away from himself. Thus, we are as surprised as she when we find him involved in a project that results in social—not individual—gains. We are doubly surprised because we have come to expect and, in many cases worship, individuality. Ours is the cult of individualism that gave birth to the Bradlees of our world.

For most Americans (and increasing numbers in the rest of the world), the search for identity is both means and end. Because it is almost totally symbolic, it is elusive and ever-changing so that we can never achieve it. The next fad or fashion puts identity further beyond our reach and we must direct increasing amounts of our energy to its pursuit.

Our never-ending quest for identity consumes two resources in scarce supply: the productive capacity of the society and the physical and emotional energy of the individual. Because these resources are absolutely essential to the attainment of social justice, individuality robs us of our capacity to address social needs. As the cancer of individualism infects other cultures, the attention of the economically active and the politically powerful is diverted from society to the self.

The misdirection of resources is clearly obvious in the symbols of individuality. The advertising messages of the leading consumer products prove the point. Clothes make the man or woman. And, if we are insensitive to fashion, we can always read the labels that cover our garments. If we feel that we are too much a part of the herd, we can always smell different by buying the latest boutique cologne. In fact, each item of consumption defines us as individual.

The symbols of identity are not only costly to the consumer. They channel productive capacity to the landfills of outdated identities. By continually changing symbols, we use up the appearance, but not the substance, of many basic products. It is ironic that even the free clothing offered by our charitable organizations is no longer acceptable to the poor. Their labels are out-of-date!

At the personal level, the damage is even greater. Individualism centers all our thinking on ourselves. We pursue income in order to acquire a newer, more expensive set of symbols. We seek power as an end in itself, not as a means to ends that might exist outside our narrow vision. Even our most personal social ties to family and friends are symbols of our individuality; else why dress our children in images of ourselves? or select friends for their position? or acquire "trophy" husbands and wives?

There is no place in the pursuit of individuality for the common good. For the individual, organizations exist only to provide the economic means whereby identity can be attained. Society exists only as a display case where individuality can be exhibited. Others exist only to admire individuality or, in special cases, to set new symbols of individuality.

When individuality penetrates business and government organizations, it twists purpose to the whims of each person. This is Robert Bellah's "utilitarian individual": the person who needs no others and is wholly centered on "number one." When these people make decisions, they are always directed at increased reward and power. In effect, they use organization resources for personal gain, not for common purpose.

These are powerful forces in our culture and they will not be easy to overturn. What inducements can we possibly offer the individual to convince him or her to work for the common goals of our organizations and our society? For many, there are no satisfactory alternatives. When identity is bound up with symbols, power, and self-indulgence, it is unlikely to be reshaped to a more socially responsible form. Instead, it is to those who have found little meaning in superficial identities that our work must be directed.

We must stand in awe of Norah, who was able to see the germ of social responsibility in Bradlee. As we think back over the earlier parables, we can see what Norah observed: Bradlee was ready to be swayed by her arguments. He was not yet lost to the cult of individuality. He was ready to find fulfillment in his considerable intellect and in its use for purposes too large to fit the individual.

One Body

The central message we bring to those around us is that we are all members of one body. We share both problems and possibilities. This biblical concept has a special meaning in modern times, when interdependency is obvious in our social and economic systems and in our environment. The meaning behind the message has never been more clear; socially centered action is the only viable course for survival. There are no other options.

Once we accept the reality of worldwide interdependence, we have a totally new perspective on identity. From this perspective, identity is defined not in symbols, but in action. A new set of symbols and rewards comes into play to assist individuals in forming socially meaningful identities.

We can take a lesson from those who are committed to fundamentalist teachings. In every one of these movements—whether Islamic, Christian, or Jewish—there is little room for individuality. Each person is valued as a member of *one body*—which defines the scope of individuality and assesses its contribution to the whole. While we may condemn the rigidity of fundamental movements, we must recognize that they have a powerful capacity to give meaning to the lives of people at all levels of society.

In the paradigm of democratic capitalism, the measure of the individual is found in the integration of money, morality, and power. Of these three, it is morality that is the "gold standard" of individual action. Morality liberates us from our hedonism and sets us on a course to redefine ourselves and our work. When we accept this new collection of measures, we open ourselves to a new paradigm of ourselves—one that makes the following changes in self-concept possible.

First, ethical behavior replaces designer jeans as a statement of self. Through ethical action, we acquire an image of substance that is clearly seen by others. These actions exhibit our values and strengthen our place in the larger community. They are easy to wear as they fit better with use and, unlike jeans, they do not fade with time. This is the garment that Bradlee has taken on; it is the chariot he rides in place of Kaiser Bill.

Second, there are greater measures of power available to those who act ethically to achieve social justice. This is not a narrow power of position; it is legitimate power given by many to those who act for the common good. Due to its legitimacy, the power we gain by ethical actions is easy to maintain. It grows naturally and is exercised with the full consent of those it directs.

The identity resulting from this shift of perspective is not only more substantial, it is more satisfying. It does not have to be defended; it is defended and supported by others. It need not follow the zigs and zags of fashion; it sets a fashion of incredible durability. It does not have to be protected; it gains its strength and appeal because it is shared. And it does not diminish those who wear it; it exalts their individual contributions to a more promising social order.

Acquiring this new identity is a matter of shifting the ground on which we measure ourselves. In the words of the Seventh Commandment:

THE SEVENTH COMMANDMENT

Cast aside the symbols of individuality and define yourself by the consequences of your action

CHAPTER NINE

The Parable of Despair: Economics, Opportunity, and Social Justice

In Norah's Wall Street everything was larger than life. Organizations were so immense that no single person knew of their scope. Trades and exchanges involved the wealth of whole governments. Decisions were locked in vast networks of consequence so that the simplest act had implications for all the world. Norah saw the magnitude of her surroundings and wondered whether they would be shaped to the good of simple men and women.

Norah's workers were similarly puzzled. They often spoke to her, saying, "We are driven by the system and are powerless to control it. We cannot be expected to foresee all things, nor can we depend upon others to act as they promise." Norah knew that their hearts were troubled and that she needs must give them direction lest they despair.

Bradlee was one of these. He was a most industrious worker and the volume of his trades was always among the highest in Norah's house. Despite his obvious success, he was unhappy. At the end of a day's trading, he would often stop by Norah's office and talk about changing his life's work.

One day, Norah asked him, "Bradlee, you are melancholy. You seem not to like your work. What is it about Wall Street that bothers you?"

Paradigms and Parables

"Oh, Norah. It all seems so futile. I try hard in my counsel and trading to seek after social justice. I try to reason with my clients as to the social consequences of their actions. But it counts for so little!"

"Why say you that?" she asked. "Do not your clients follow your counsel? Do not many unfortunate persons have a better life due to your acts?"

"Possibly some few do. But other events overpower me every day. Even this month, I counseled a client not to invest in Honeywell as they continue to manufacture instruments of death. No sooner had I done this than the stock rose and my client lost. Now my advice is of little value to her."

"Bradlee, you must have faith that yours is the right path. Nowhere is it written that the road to social justice is paved with gold, nor that the decisions to act ethically are without risk."

Bradlee nodded in agreement at her advice. "What you say is true, Norah. But the systems are so large and I am so small. What is the worth of my pitiful contributions?"

She answered him, saying, "The actions you take are of inestimable worth! You have gained in the value you set on yourself. Have you not taken great pride in the housing project you have set forth in Brooklyn?"

"That is so," he agreed, "but it is in the larger market where so much is wrong that I feel powerless."

"So do we all. Nonetheless, as we grow in number, the power we have for doing good increases manyfold. Have not our works already resulted in companies making better products for the good of our customers?"

"Yes, that is so. It is not in the small things of commerce where we fail. It is in the larger arena of international affairs where we count for so little."

"I cannot agree," she said. "Did not our counsel result in the First Bank writing down its third-world loans? Will not this produce a better life for those living in poverty?"

"In some measure, I suppose so. But what of the instruments of death? Has not their trade increased? Are not many of the same unfortunates victims of these products?"

"Verily, the trade is larger. But its increase has gone hand in hand with greed. Is not our Congress examining frauds among those who make and procure these things? Is there not a change in world opinion that goes against this trade?"

"But what of Honeywell, Norah? Have I not failed my client?"

"That you have not. In today's Journal we see that Honeywell is losing many millions. And these losses are due to the selfsame instruments you abhor. Your client should take comfort in her choice of a wise counselor!"

Bradlee rose from his chair and bowed to Norah. "Once again you have seen through the confusion of our work to its clear end. You have affirmed my faith in economic justice."

Norah answered, "You have hit on the key, Bradlee; it is faith that will make us successful in the long run. Our systems can be made to work for all, but only if we at the centers of power have their interests in mind at all times."

Grieving for the World's Children

Bradlee's feeling of despair is one we all share when we confront the magnitude of the social problems we now face. Consider the fate of children in the third world. In December of 1988, the United Nations issued its annual report on the status of the world's children. In that year, 14 million children died of various health-related conditions. These data were especially alarming in that the recent down-trend in child mortality has been reversed and is on the increase. This is especially true in third-world countries where recent gains in public health practices and parent education are gravely at risk. There is cause for despair unless problems like those facing children have an audience among those with social and economic power.

The plight of the world's children is a moral problem which is coming to rest on the desks of business and political leaders in the developed nations. It is a problem for business since at least a half million of these deaths can be traced to changes in health and education in debtor nations. The interest burden of third-world debt is now so great that it cannot be serviced without seriously depleting the social programs so badly needed by disadvantaged people. Social justice is clearly economic justice. And, as usual, when economic pressures are applied to governments, it is women and children who suffer.

The worldwide crisis in children's health and well-being is but another instance of what happens when we separate social and moral problems from economics. The social injustices of our time are not the separate concerns of churches and governments; they are the consequences of actions taken in the world's boardrooms. Since most of these councils sit in the United States, it is our own business community that must take responsibility for the measures of injustice allotted to the world's unfortunate.

The nature of our responsibility for social justice has been given a clear focus in the 1986 Pastoral Letter of the U.S. Catholic Bishops. The first sentence of their message reads, "Every perspective on economic life that is human, moral, and Christian must be shaped by three questions: What does the economy do for people? What does it do to people? And how do they participate in it?" These are broader questions than the ethical issues we have raised in this book. They cut to the center of our moral commitments to others and help us to define the interests we share with all the people of the world.

What the bishops are saying is that economics, opportunity, and social justice are the key elements in the functioning of contemporary global society. They have added to the simple drawing we used in Chapter 1 so that it looks like this:

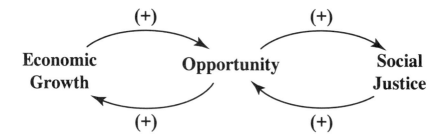

When we put social justice in the picture, we have added the motivational "driver" to economy and opportunity. It works this way. As opportunity increases, so does social justice. When it does, the "drive" kicks in and more people are motivated to participate in the economy—which leads to more economic growth. And the whole process grows without end.

But—and here's the important point—it can also work the other way. If, for any reason, one of these three variables decreases, those decreases are passed around the loops and all variables are reduced. For instance, if opportunity is diminished, so will social justice be decreased. This will reduce the motivation of people to engage the economy, and economic growth will decline. These effects, if unchecked, will multiply around the loop and the seeds of social disaster will have sprouted.

It's the job of business leaders to make these loops work for people. This is an imperative that cannot be stated in soft language; business men and women must take personal responsibility for the morality of their actions. Each of us is compelled by social necessity to look beyond the ethical implications of our actions in the arena where we work to the morality of our behavior in a world context. This means that we cannot evaluate our actions only by the standards of ethical conduct within our organizations and communities. In addition, we need to anticipate how our decisions and products will affect all humankind and we will need to find mechanisms to allow those who are affected to participate in the economic activities we are managing.

The Pastoral Letter gives us a perspective that can help to assure the larger morality of our work. The six principles laid down by the bishops can be readily applied to the normal course of business activity.

Economy, Opportunity, and Social Justice

1. "Every economic decision and institution must be judged in light of whether it protects or undermines the dignity of the human person."

    This principle expands our view of the corporate bottom line to include those who are outside the organization, but may be touched by what it does or the things it produces. In the case of the world's children, it is international banking which is very much in the moral spotlight. Unless third-world debt is restructured on a massive scale—or forgiven—hunger, illness, and death will continue to increase in debtor nations. Thus, a new investment policy is called for: one that will nurture these fragile economies so that they can achieve a measure of social justice for their people.

2. "Human dignity can be realized and protected only in community."

This principle takes the problem of individuality to a world scale. We are one with the starving mother in Sudan as much as we are one with our lunch partner on Wall Street. We must come to realize that the suffering of the most remote person diminishes our humanity and that resources are to be used for the common good and not for personal gratification. This is a message that ethical business leaders must continually spread among their colleagues if concentrated economic power is to result in social justice.

3. "All people have the right to participate in the economic life of society."

Here is a principle that challenges our imagination. Not every individual can be present at the councils of business and government. Instead, decision makers must represent the interests of the less powerful if they are to have the opportunity to benefit from the economic system. This may be as simple as providing corporate child care to assist single parents in holding jobs. Or, it may be as complex as deciding which products will be offered for sale in a third-world country and how advertising might shape consumer behavior to the benefit or detriment of the individual.

4. "All members of the society have a special obligation to the poor and vulnerable."

Business leaders have come face to face with this imperative in recent years. Legislation that provides for equal treatment of handicapped workers, advertising controls that protect the uninformed buyer, and pressures for corporate social responsibility are all examples of this principle in action. They do not, however, go far enough. What is required is a more aggressive stance on the part of the corporation and its leaders to ensure social justice for the poor.

5. "Human rights are the minimum condition for life in community."

These rights include life, food, clothing, shelter, rest, medical care, education, and employment. They cannot be achieved without involvement in the economic system. When we exclude vast numbers of minority youth from employment due to inadequate education, we are violating their human rights. What this principle implies is that we must ensure that everyone in our economic system has the opportunities we have secured for our own children. This does not guarantee equality of outcomes; it does mandate equality of opportunity.

6. "Society as a whole, acting through public and private institutions, has the moral responsibility to enhance human dignity and protect human rights."

In our world society, it is not the individual, but the organization that will determine the course of social justice. No single business leader can change the accounts of third-world debt; no individual marketer can decide what is to be sold to the poor; no one personnel officer can guarantee opportunity. We must act as a community to structure our organizations and institutions to offer these assurances to everyone.

Global Restructuring for Opportunity

Principles like those put forward by the bishops are generally ignored in the daily activities of governments and businesses. They are high-minded statements that make us feel good, but rarely have much to do with how we conduct our business and our lives. Despite the rather dismal history of such calls to action, we feel that there is a *global restructuring* under way, a realignment of economic power that will have dramatic effects on opportunity for much of the world's people. Powerful forces are at work that are causing *restructuring*—forces that cannot be overlooked or opposed.

Mobility: Foremost among the pressures for *restructuring* is the increasing mobility of those seeking opportunity. It is no longer possible to lock the unfortunate out of islands of economic activity. Borders and immigration controls are historical fictions that are powerless to stem the tide of migrants fleeing poverty and despair.

At the moment, it is in the European Community where this dynamic is most evident. The residents of the former Soviet Union can easily see the opportunities in the EC, and they can just as easily cross borders to get at them. In Germany alone, the 1980s were a time of exponential growth in the numbers of asylum applications. According to the Inter-Governmental Consultation on Asylum, the number of applications in Germany has increased from virtually zero to a half-million in the last ten years.

These are numbers on a scale that cannot be ignored. If these new residents are not integrated into the society and economy, they will amount to an unsustainable drain on social services. Business and government leaders have no option but to address mobility up front—by recognizing the link between economy, opportunity, and social justice.

Free trade: Trade is a force that is central to *restructuring*. It is a solution to the pressures of mobility because it can create opportunity so that people can stay at home. We can already see this at work as Mexican immigrants begin to return to a newly industrialized Mexico. California has, for example, experienced the effects of this dynamic directly. In the last five years, it has lost over 700 businesses—150 of them to Mexico. And these businesses have taken workers with them.

The common business response to free trade is to calculate its consequences in narrow gains and losses. Surely, California lost business. But it gained in reduced migration pressures on its social services. In the longer run, the balance between population and opportunity on both sides of its borders with Mexico will forge a new partnership—one in which mutual advantages take the place of exploitation.

Information: The third dynamic driving *restructuring* is the free flow of information around the globe. Information is becoming a freely traded commodity that can be put to use by any individual or organization. Networks of computers and their telecommunications links provide a real-time web on which *restructuring* is taking place.

Free communication across cultures makes it possible, for the first time in history, for world citizenship to evolve. As people begin to identify their common interests in opportunity, economic growth, and social justice, they can utilize communication networks to shape their activities to these ends. To the extent that information continues to be freely traded, there is hope that *restructuring* will result in continued improvement in the quality of life of all the world's people.

Money, Morality, and Power Revisited

The Eighth Commandment is about the bonds that unite money, morality, and power. It speaks of the necessity for economic growth to produce resources (money) for the common good. The commandment urges us to recognize that economy is the principle force (power) for generating opportunity. And it faces us with the fact that social justice (morality) is *the* end toward which all of us must strive.

THE EIGHTH COMMANDMENT

Recognize that economy, opportunity, and social justice are the legs on which world society stands

CHAPTER 10

The Parable of the Gift: In Search of Extravagance

The people of Norah's time were much taken with display. At the Holiday Season of the year, they would shower gifts of great cost on themselves—and a few others. Price counted for the most in these exchanges. Those who were very rich and powerful would give extravagant gifts; those of lesser means must content themselves with shoddy goods. For the gift itself was what was important to them.

Norah much regretted these practices, for they represented that which was most false in her society. When it came time to exchange gifts at her place of business, she took care to select an object that embodied much thought. She cared little for cost and set no store by extravagance.

Bradlee was not like her. For him, commerce set the value of all gifts. Try as he might, he could not break away from these patterns of thought. One Holiday, he came into Norah's office taking care to conceal an object behind his back.

When Norah looked up to him, he said, "Norah, you have done much for me this year. You have shown me many errors in my thinking. For this I am grateful and would show my appreciation by a token. Would this be acceptable to you?"

Norah smiled and answered, "Bradlee, I have taken great pleasure in working with you this year. If you wish to commemorate our relationship, by all means give me this token."

At this, he brought forth a small box inscribed with the name "Cartier."

Norah exclaimed at its simple beauty and opened it carefully. There, lying in splendor on a white cushion, was a pin of extravagant design.

She look into Bradlee's eyes. "Bradlee, this is a thing of great beauty and great cost. I could not accept such a thing, for it speaks of money more than feeling. Does it not seem to do so in your eyes?"

Bradlee was puzzled. "Why, yes, I suppose so. But how else can I show my appreciation for all that you have done for me?"

"Consider this," she said, "have you not changed your view of business? Do not you measure your accomplishments in new ways? Answer me this."

"That is so. It is the very reason I wished to give this gift to you. You have given me a new perspective on business. For the first time, it is meaningful to me and I feel that each day's work is of some value to others."

"Verily, that is so. You have changed and I have taken great pleasure in watching your progress. Make no mistake, it is yourself that has made these changes. I have but questioned your reasons and provided a foil for your explanations."

"Norah. It has been much more than that! You have clearly been my guide. Without you, I would have been even more centered on myself. Come, accept this gift as a token of my gratitude."

"Bradlee, we need no tokens between us. I understand your needs and your strengths. You have already given a gift of great extravagance. A gift that is without price in the marketplace."

"What is that?" he asked.

"It is the gift of your commitment to right action and social justice. Your growing faith in the power of business for good and your capacity to shape its work to the ends of justice is a gift I greatly treasure."

He smiled and put the box into his pocket. "Again, you are right, Norah. When I purchased this gift, I felt that I was measuring by a wrong standard. Yet, I could not be content with actions alone to show my feeling."

"Let me say to you again, Bradlee, you are the extravagant gift! Without measure, for your commitment grows in value with time and it gives pleasure to many. Is that not what the Lord would have us do with our lives?"

"Forsooth, Norah, you have said it well. Let us go forth and return this bauble and together use the funds to a purpose we both shall choose."

In Search of Extravagance

We can talk about our collective efforts; we can attempt to move our corporations toward the achievement of economic justice; we can hope that the governments of the world will see the futility of narrow nationalism. But ethical actions and social justice all come down to our behavior as individuals. Without individual commitment to these goals, no amount of institutional or group effort will achieve justice for those most in need.

Once we recognize the imperative of social justice, we are compelled to make the extravagant gift of our commitment to its achievement. It is an extravagant gift because, like Bradlee, we must change our ways of evaluating ourselves, our work, and our colleagues.

You may find yourself a bit uneasy at the use of the word *extravagant* in this context. The word may cause you to think of "that which is more than is needed." Such is not the case. The extravagant gift of your commitment is like some other gifts, which Annie Dillard catalogs in her insightful book *Pilgrim at Tinker Creek*. She writes:

"The extravagant gesture is the very stuff of creation. After the one extravagant gesture of creation in the first place, the universe has continued to deal exclusively in extravagance, flinging intricacies and colossi down aeons of emptiness heaping profusions on profligacies with every fresh vigor. The whole show has been on fire from the word go!" (1974, p. 9).

Although our individual gifts cannot be measured on the cosmic scale of creation, they are extravagant in our own frame of reference. Our commitment is the most we have to give. It is recognition that we live in a world of choice. We may walk the yellow brick road, the primrose path, the straight and narrow, or the road to destruction. There is the boulevard of broken dreams and easy street; the high road and the low. There is MY way and the Way of Commitment. Each of these paths sets our feet on our personal journey. They bound our actions so that one deed flows from another, without our conscious direction.

To deviate from these familiar pathways is indeed an extravagant gift. Reflect, for a moment, on the changes we have seen in Bradlee. His whole frame of reference has expanded to include both a new view of society and a new personal identity. When we commit ourselves to the attainment of social justice, we are setting out on a new course of action, a new way of living that is neither easy nor predetermined.

The extravagant gift is a recognition of the finite nature of our lives and the fact that what we do may or may not contribute to the attainment of social justice. We may accomplish a great deal or nothing at all. We may walk alone or with others. We may be creator or catalyst. We may be remembered far into the future or forgotten in an instant. But when we make the extravagant gift of our commitment, we are binding ourselves to the course of humanity and are, in our extravagance, increasing the probabilities of justice for all people.

The extravagant gift is, ultimately, about our relationship to God. It is a recognition that God has done nothing to us. We have done unto each other. Colleen McCullough, in her *Creed for a Third Millennium,* has suggested:

> The main reason such vast numbers of people have abandoned God in the last 150 years, is not actually to do with God at all. It is to do with human beings. If God expects anything at all of us, then he simply expects us, with patience and endurance and strength, to overcome every obstacle, not he, but we, ourselves, and our environment keep putting in our own way. This is not God's world. It is our world. God gave it to us. I cannot believe in a proprietarial God. We have made this world what it is. We should not blame him for what we have made of it. I like to think that when we die, the best part of us goes back to God, not necessarily as the entity we call self, but as the part of God already in us. That lowly spirit. But I don't know, and I can't tell you. I must believe that inside me is a little drop of God to fuel me and keep me going. What

Chapter 10: The Parable of the Gift

I do most certainly know is that here is where I am right now, here in this world made by me and my fellow men, and all of our ancestors. The world which is therefore, my responsibility as it is all men's responsibility" (1985, p. 57).

By accepting this responsibility we are setting the basis for the extravagant gift—the potential for changing and improving world society. Commitment provides an arena in which our imagination can function; where new solutions can abound; where a collective spirit can dominate our problems. The extravagant gift converts us to a new use of imagination.

According to Paul Ricoeur, this is a conversion to a new set of images of ourselves and the world. "Every real conversion is first a revolution of the level of our directive images. By changing his imagination, man alters his existence. The imagination, insofar as it seeks out the most impossible potentialities of man, is the advance outpost of mankind, marching toward greater lucidity and maturity" (1965, p. 127).

In giving the extravagant gift, we, in effect, go beyond ourselves, beyond the limits of banal reality, and into the imaginative world of creative acts of confidence in order to make the very best future. We alter the way we look at reality. We become more selective in our choice of models for our action, being certain that our model is more like Jesus than Cassius. In the same way, our social model is more like the simple communities of ordinary peoples than like the opulence of ancient Rome.

Choosing the proper models will make us revolutionaries in our culture. The kind of commitment Jesus spoke of is not to be found at Club Med, nor in the rituals of the New York Stock Exchange. It is in our own actions and the consequences they produce. Can there be a better model than Mother Teresa, whose loving acts of commitment to caring for the poorest of the poor, the weathliest of the dying, seem not to make a difference in the macrocosm of the earth? Does her and her sisters' care for those few hundreds of dying wretches make a scratch in the poverty and death in a world that numbers more than five million such wretches?

You know the answer to that.

The work of Mother Teresa and others like her is living testimony to the power of the Ninth Commandment.

THE NINTH COMMANDMENT

Give the extravagant gift of your commitment to social justice

CHAPTER 11

The Parable Of Ethics: One World

On feast days–and many other days–the men of Wall Street would gather together for fellowship. They would discourse on trade, review the events of the week, admire the latest happenings in sport, and talk of the business of their employers. This was called "The Three-Martini Lunch." Bradlee was one of those who found much pleasure in these days.

One afternoon, at his return, Norah observed him pass her office. He seemed poor in spirit, so after a time, she went to his station to inquire after his affliction.

"Bradlee, my friend, it seemeth to me that you are downcast. What is it that troubles thee?"

"Oh, Norah! It is nothing. It will pass," he answered.

"Come, Bradlee. It is unlike you to be thus. Tell me of your concern that I might counsel thee."

"It was our feast this day. I spoke in anger to my friends and they no longer desire my company. They drove me from the hall!"

"Bradlee! How terrible! And how unlike you. What was it that angered thee?"

"The others at our feast were discussing trades and I was but a listener. They spoke of a forthcoming buyout of Basic Products."

"I had heard of this. But did not the offer fall through?"

"That is what I had thought. But there is a new buyer from another Nation who is about to make an offer that will triple the value of Basic stock."

"That is indeed interesting. It is probably but a rumor. Have we not heard this many times before? And have not all offers come to naught?"

"Verily they have. But the counting house of my friends has arranged a secret meeting between the new buyer and the trustees of Basic. It is now a friendly takeover."

"That is indeed news! You were right. When others hear of this, the price of Basic stock will rise threefold. But how could that anger thee, Bradlee?"

"Forsooth, Norah. It was my friends. They did conspire to trade on this news. Those from another house agreed to buy great quantities of stock for our fellowship to hold and sell when prices rise."

"Bradlee! That is insider trading and most unethical!"

"I know this, Norah. And I did so tell my friends. They greeted my statement with laughter!"

"That is their shame! What then did you do?"

"I told them that I would not be a part of their plan. This angered them, but not as much as what I then said. I told them that I would watch trading in Basic Products stock until the buyout is announced. If I saw that there were large trades from their houses, I would come to their managers and so inform them."

"Bradlee, I take great pride in what you have done! You have acted as an ethical trader must."

"But Norah, my friends feel betrayed! They no longer will feast with me! They have cast me from our fellowship!"

"Come, Bradlee. You have achieved much more than you lost. You have grown in stature by your ethical actions. If your friends cannot see this, they are false. Think on this. What you have done will shine forth in their minds.

As time passes, many of them will come to see what you have taught them and they will praise you for showing them the way."

At this, she held out her hands to him and raised him up from his chair. They then went forth from the counting house.

And that was but the beginning.

One World

When we bring our faith and commitment together, when we unite our future with the futures of all other people, we unleash the potential for a world where economic and social justice can be realized. How does this relate to our individual actions? How does a unity of faith and finance bring about a better future? How is our commitment made to count for others?

These are the questions we can imagine Bradlee asking himself. In this parable, he has made the ultimate choice—selecting ethical behavior over friendship. When we make choices of this magnitude, we need some answers.

As Norah tells Bradlee, answers come to us in time through the unfolding of the consequences of our actions. As our many individual acts are concatenated over time, they do "add up" to a new world scenario.

Think of a typical concatenation. When we invest a thousand dollars in a new stock offering, we help make it possible for a company to employ workers. These people take their wages into the community where they buy groceries, cars, and other products—which, in turn, provides jobs for people who also need food and transportation. All these people pay taxes, which go for government programs and services. This is concatenation writ large by its multiplication in the economic system.

But what has all this to do with creating a better future? Just this: each of our present acts has an incalculable effect in the future. If in this present moment, I act ethically in my dealings with another, my action becomes part of that person—as does an act of greed or self-interest. My actions may combine with those of others, done or undone, to create a new future for the recipient.

When Bradlee's friends reflect on his ethical behavior, they will surely be influenced by what he has done. And their future actions will be shaped, in part, by the stand he has taken.

If we could suspend ourselves at some vantage point above the earth and observe just one human life, we would see Divine Providence combine with free will and concatenation. We would see people interacting with one another; we would see their behavior building over time through concatenation. The thread of the human condition runs through what we see. We would see this condition improve or worsen depending upon the extent to which the actors we are watching guide their behavior by the principles of ethics and justice. Their actions truly change the course of the world.

Is it possible to continue those business practices that lead us away from social and economic justice? Of course. Every choice of the unethical is just that. And these choices change the world, too. Clearly, the big moments in business raise ethical questions. Decisions about new products, new plant locations, new policies can be readily analyzed as to their impact on social justice. But concatenation tells us that the little decisions grow into big ones. And they count up to changed futures as they work through the human networks in the corporation and the community.

Peace and Prosperity: The Big Picture

Parables, Paradigms, and Commandments have a great deal to do with Wall Street. As discussed in this book, they are not narrow religious terms, dependent on the definitions of particular denominations. Rather, they are concepts that arise from each of us as human beings. Incomplete understanding of their meaning and implications in the business world has made Wall Street a threat to humanity in this century.

Ethical thinking and acting must be brought out of the cloister and made relevant to business life. We must "Talk the talk of social justice" and "Walk the walk of social action." The case for an integration of faith and finance is clear. Business leaders who have faith in the future of people must give the extravagant gift of commitment to using financial power for the good of all people. Each of us who helps control the world's economic systems must reiterate our acceptance of the commandments that shape ethical conduct. By realizing that we are all part of one world, we can help one another to make it a better place.

The end result of business activity centered on social justice is to deliver prosperity to all people and to ensure peace among them. Business leaders must understand that this noble objective is also in their own best interests. For without peace and prosperity, the world is a very dangerous place, one where organizations and individuals are at risk. The truth of this relationship is evident in the bombed-out hotels in Iran and Iraq. It is reaffirmed in the escalating violence in South Africa. And it is a dynamic that is at work wherever social justice takes second place to greed.

The concatenation of the words we have been using in this book—Opportunity, Social Justice, Peace, Prosperity—adds up to a new paradigm for business. It is a people-centered paradigm that replaces individuality; it is a paradigm in which action is driven by ethics not greed; and it is a way of looking at the world as a whole and the role of business in making it a better place. In sum, this paradigm is one that the wise business leader accepts as the only viable course of action.

Consider Jennifer Trusted's inspired words, and make them a part of each moment of each portion of your life: "It is the wise who know that to act morally is to fulfill the aspirations of human nature; this knowledge is, indeed, what makes them wise" (1987).

The essence of wisdom is embodied in the Tenth Commandment:

THE TENTH COMMANDMENT

Remember: Peace and prosperity in all the world are created by ethical business practice

References

Batra, R. 1988. *Surviving the Great Depression of 1990.* New York: Simon and Schuster.

Benjamin, W. 1988. "That's Jobs, Not Job." *Corporate Report Minnesota* (February): 21–13.

Bowen, E. 1987. "Looking to Its Roots." *Time* (25 May): 26–29.

Brzezinski, Z. 1988. *The Grand Failure: The Birth and Death of Communism in the 20th Century.* New York: Scribners.

Conoco Oil Co. 1976. *The Conoco Conscience.* New York: Continental Oil Co.

DeThomasis, L. 1984. *My Father's Business.* Westminster, MD: Christian Classics.

———— W. Ammentorp, and M. Fox. 1991. *The Transformal Organization.* Winona, MN: The Metnoia Group.

Dillard, A. 1974. *Pilgrim at Tinker Creek.* New York: Harper.

Drucker, P. 1987. "The Transnational Economy." *Wall Street Journal* (25 August): 30.

Dubaski, J. 1989. "The Do-Gooder." *Financial World* (27 June 27): 70.

Etzioni, A. 1989. "Good Ethics is Good Business—Really." *Wall Street Journal* (12 February): 2.

Gilder, G. 1988. "Tied to the Masts of Their Fortunes." *Forbes* (24 October): 348–50.

Goodpaster, K. and J. Matthews. 1982. "Can a Corporation Have a Conscience?" *Harvard Business Review* (January): 132–41.

Hall, E. 1976. *Beyond Culture.* Garden City, NY: Doubleday.

Jones, D., ed. 1982. *Doing Ethics in Business.* Cambridge, MA: Gunn and Hain.

Kelly, W. 1972. *Pogo: We Have Met the Enemy and He Is Us.* New York: Simon and Schuster.

Kindel, S. 1989. "Bad Apple for Baby." *Financial World* (27 June): 48.

Kinsley, M. 1985. "Perot as Robin Hood: Take from the Rich, Educate the Poor." *Wall Street Journal* (30 May): 27.

Kuhn, T. 1970. *The Structure of Scientific Revolutions.* Chicago: University of Chicago Press.

McCullough, C. 1985. *Creed for a Third Millennium.* New York: Harper and Row.

McGurn, W. 1985. "To Live and Die For A Dogma." *The Wall Street Journal* (19 July): 12.

McNeill, W.C. 1990. "Fundamentalisms and the World of the 1990's." In Marty, M. and Appleby, R.S. (eds), *Fundamentalisms and Society.* Chicago: University of Chicago Press.

Meadows, D., et al. 1993. *Beyond the Limits.* Post Mills, VT: Chelsea Green.

Minogue, K. 1985. *Alien Powers: The Pure Theory of Ideology.* New York: St. Martin's Press.

Murchland, B. 1984. *Humanism and Capitalism.* Washington, DC: Enterprise Institute.

Olson, M. 1988. "The Social Costs of Economic Growth." *The Wall Street Journal* (22 December): A12.

Polander, E., and J. Jackson. 1988. "The Social Contract Between Business and Society in Constitutional Perspective." *Proteus* 5 (2): 23–32.

Prodhoretz, N. 1982. "The New Defenders of Capitalism." *Harvard Business Review* (March): 97–101.

Ricoeur, P. 1965. *History and Truth: The Image of God and the Epic of Man.* Evanston, IL: Northwestern University Press.

Ryan, L. 1988. "The Wave of the Future." *The Tablet* 10: 1423–25.

Schillebeeckx, E. 1987. *Jesus in Our Western Culture.* London: SCM Press.

Storkey, A. 1986. *Transforming Economics.* London: Third Way Books.

Tamari, M. 1987. *With All Your Possessions.* New York: Free Press.

Trusted, J. 1987. *Moral Principles and Social Values.* London: Routledge and Kegan Paul Ltd.

Wallace, D., and J. White. 1988. "Building Integrity in Organizations." *New Management* (6) 1: 30–35.

Wartzman, R. 1987. "Nature or Nurture? Study Blames Ethical Lapses on Corporate Goals." *The Wall Street Journal* (6 October).

Wilder, G. 1988. "Thinking Ethically." *Issues in Ethics* 1 (2): 2–3.

APPENDIX

The Ten Commandments for Doing Ethics in Business

I. TALK THE TALK OF SOCIAL JUSTICE.

II. WALK THE WALK OF SOCIAL ACTION.

III. PUT PEOPLE ON THE BOTTOM LINE OF CORPORATE CALCULATION.

IV. DO RIGHT YOURSELF, DON'T LEAVE IT TO GOD.

V. DO WHAT IS ETHICAL, AND YOU WILL DO GOOD BUSINESS.

VI. LET YOUR WORK INTEGRATE FAITH AND FINANCE.

VII. CAST ASIDE THE SYMBOLS OF INDIVIDUALITY AND DEFINE YOURSELF BY THE CONSEQUENCES OF YOUR ACTION.

VIII. RECOGNIZE THAT ECONOMY, OPPORTUNITY, AND SOCIAL JUSTICE ARE THE LEGS ON WHICH WORLD SOCIETY STANDS.

IX. GIVE THE EXTRAVAGANT GIFT OF YOUR COMMITMENT TO SOCIAL JUSTICE.

X. REMEMBER: PEACE AND PROSPERITY IN ALL THE WORLD ARE CREATED BY ETHICAL BUSINESS PRACTICE.